PASS IT ON

Live long, laugh often, love much!
God bless —
        Berenice Denton

Pass It On

WILD TALES AND ESTATE SALES

OF BERENICE DENTON

WITH

JADYN M. STEVENS

Pass It On

Cover & book design by Jadyn M. Stevens / Eveready Press

A deep appreciation of and special thanks to Carole Baker Koonce for heading the research, interview process and production of an original manuscript which served as the basis for this book.

Excerpts by Charles and Ann Wells, used by permission.

Cover photo by Rocky Alvey

Printed in the USA

ISBN: 978-0-9837256-4-0

EVEREADY PRESS
1817 Broadway Nashville, TN 37203

To Jimmy and my children

Yesterday's successes belong to yesterday,
with all of yesterday's defeats and sorrows.
The day is here,
the time is now.

Thank God for new responsibilities
that help me grow and for the love
of others that keeps me going.

All progress grows out of discontent
with things as they are.

Next to knowing when to seize an opportunity,
the most important thing in life is to know
when to take advantage of it.

Iron sharpeneth iron; so a man sharpeneth
the countenence of his friend.
Proverbs 27:17

FOREWORD

LET ME BEGIN by saying...

We all spend too much time fretting about what we overlooked or failed to accomplish in the past. We overload ourselves with worry about what will happen in the future. The important thing is to live in the present, and make it count to the fullest of our abilities. In so doing, we may well bring a blessing to someone else and enhance our own lives.

So don't chunk your junk, don't miss the fun of rumaging through the attic or searching for treasure in a long unused closet. Don't forget you could also find in a basement items of special value. Come along and join me on my wild and hilarious journey. It is truly filled with God's blessings.

Berenice Denton

Thank You...

TO MY STAFF in "the field" and at the shop's office. Your tireless efforts and dedication mean so much to me. Thank you Mandy Smith, Lora Vandervoort, Simone Marshall, Ed Arnett, Annie Bolan and Helen Currie.

Thank You...

MY DEAR FRIENDS Carole Baker and Gardner Smith whose loving efforts helped get this adventure in ink started.

ANN WELLS
INTRODUCES BERENICE

CENTENNIAL CLUB
APRIL 4, 2003

THIS INTRODUCTION HAS two parts: professional and personal. Professionally, Berenice Denton, who has been called the "Estate Sale Queen," manages estate sales, appraisals, garage sales, relocating, and consignment sales. She has attended seminars given by the Appraisers Association of America and Christie's, and she is a member of the American Appraisers Association of America, Inc. The list of her accomplishments and activities in the antiques and appraisals field goes on at length. They all prove how capable, how well qualified, and how successful she is. In fact, as one friend said, "The fact of the matter is, she's an extraordinary businesswoman."

Now the personal: I met Berenice Miller in 1946 when she joined our fourth grade class at Parmer School. She made an instant hit. Before long she became my best friend. Only later did I realize that everyone else also thought that she was their best friend. Our teacher Miss Corbitt was a formidable lady and she never smiled. She demanded total attention and she demanded perfection. She got neither from Berenice. On the first day of school, when we had written our names on our papers, she said, "Bernice! That's not the way to spell your name. Bernice is not spelled B-e-r-e-n-i-c-e."

"That's the way I spell it," Berenice responded. "Well then, replied Miss Corbitt, "bring me a note from your mother tomorrow."

The next day, of course, Mrs. Miller backed up the spelling of B-e-r-e-n-i-c-e as correct. Miss Corbitt had met her match.

There were many such episodes during Berenice's years at Parmer. In eighth grade, she told our teacher that, since she lived nearby, she had permission to go home for lunch and to take a friend with her. The teacher was so startled and Berenice so full of authority, that we went to her house for lunch, quite proud of ourselves. The next morning, the teacher and Mrs. Talley, the principal, announced that no one was permitted, ever again, to go home for lunch.

In 2001 our Lunch Bunch celebrated our birthdays by spending several days in New Orleans. We had many wonderful experiences, but my favorite was on the evening we went to a nightspot that had loud, typical New Orleans music. We all asked them to play "'When the Saints Go Marching In." Finally, they did, and as the music reached a crescendo, Berenice jumped up, wrapped a scarf around her head, and started marching and dancing around that room. I've always been fairly proper and reserved, but Berenice brings out the mischief in me, as she does in us all. So I jumped up - we all did - as Berenice led us in singing, waving our arms, and marching around the room to the sounds of "When the Saints Go Marching In."

We could tell Berenice stories on and on, but Berenice is much more than a collection of funny stories. At heart, she is a friendly, loving person. She enjoys meeting and knowing all kinds of people, and she is the most loyal of friends. "Once a friend, always a friend" could be her motto. She has boundless energy, and she can pack more into a twenty-four hour day than anyone anywhere. And if she gets into a predicament, she can always talk herself out of it.

Her most important assets are her strong faith in God and her family. "I have Jimmy and our four children and our thirteen grandchildren," she says. "They are my most precious treasures."

I'd like to tell you about a vision I have of Berenice many years in the future. I can almost see her prancing through the Pearly Gates. "Just a minute now," she will say to the angel leading the way, "my phone is ringing. I won't be a minute." When she answers, it will be Jimmy Denton, who will say, "Wait for me, Berenice, I couldn't live with you, but I can't live without you. Wait for me, I'm coming." And as she enters a beautiful heaven, she will see many old friends, and she will say, "Why there's that sweet little lady I saw at all my sales, and there's that truck driver who thought I really was a 'Wild Thing' and there's Little Miss Corbitt, with a big smile on her face!" Soon she will have all of them, plus all the angels, smiling and organized, and she may even find ornaments to sell to the angels to decorate their wings. And after she has met all the people she didn't know, each one will say "That Berenice is great. She's my best friend." And then she will find a marching band, and she will arrange all her heavenly friends into a line, and she will find a scarf to wrap around her head, and she will lead that heavenly choir as they march and sing and shout "When the Saints Go Marching In."

TABLE OF CONTENTS

CHAPTER

Wild Thing
and the
Panty Snatcher

═══════

LIVING IN THE MOMENT means facing the chaotic mayhem that often accompanies such spirited goings on. I suppose this could be caused by a lack of planning, or an overt inattention to detail. I have been accused of throwing myself headlong into more than the occasional situation. I have to admit, there may be something to this... but then again, I do love the adventure of it all and who can be bothered with details with such grand things afoot?

One Christmas I was taken with a festive gem that seemed to have endless local demand. Real candy cane baskets, complete with red and white stripes that twisted into a decorative handle, made a useable and edible treat. It was a hot seller at Christmas Village and in my shop. Through friends, an opportunity arose to sell a sizeable batch to several stores in Birmingham. I planned to then go on to the Tri Delt house at the University of Alabama to visit and deliver some baskets to my daughters, Debbie and Kathy; I was determined to make it all work.

I borrowed a friend's "woody" station wagon, so called for the wood panels that ran down both sides. I filled it to the brim with boxes of the striped treasures. The order was for two hundred baskets. We still had several of the candy cane creations to load once the wagon was full, so I decided to strap them to the roof of the woody with a tarpaulin covering everything. What could go wrong?

I rolled on in my station wagon on loan with the lumpy green tarp lashed to my roof holding down several boxes with four baskets each. I was tooling along, nearly half way to Birmingham when I heard a loud "Thwump!" and then another. "What on earth," I muttered. Maybe something was wrong with the station wagon. Then another loud "Thwump!" I looked in my side mirror, as I could not see anything in the rear view mirror, and to my horror I saw one of the boxes of four carefully packed, delicate candy cane baskets skidding on the asphalt. Then a flapping noise began from above. It sounded like a giant bird was attacking my precious baskets! Thwump! Another box sailed from the roof - the tarpaulin had come loose. All I could do was grip the steering wheel and look for a place to pull off. With each box that flew off, all I could do was calculate my loss-$40.00 per box!

I rolled to a stop on the shoulder, still gripping the steering wheel. There was an ominous sky. I thought of the red mess spreading all over the car if it rained. I stared straight forward; my eyes open wide in panic. Just then my CB radio crackled to life, bringing me from my frozen state. With a shaky hand I reached for the receiver, pressed the button and with a small voice said, "This is Wild Thing. I need help. Is anybody out there? Anybody with children? Children would help!" I guess I was thinking someone with children would be a safe bet for help, but in truth, I was in no position to be choosy. The interstate was desolate. It seemed no one was around to help at all. I had chosen "Wild Thing," as my CB handle, some time before then with affirmation from Jimmy and friends that it was fitting.

A roll of thunder grumbled in the distance. Deep purple clouds gathered in the sky ahead. I noticed it was growing ever more dark; rain was coming. If the boxes got wet, I'd have peppermint melting into a sticky syrup oozing down my dear friend's station wagon. I imagined myself driving home in a red and white, peppermint-covered woody having lost many of my baskets to the road and the rain. I was at the end of me, so I turned to prayer. I asked the good Lord above to send someone nice to help me.

The CB radio startled me as a gravelly voice burst forth from the 3 inch, dust-covered speaker.

"I got ya covered, Wild Thang. This is Night Crawler... and ehhh... (long pause) sometimes they call me Panty Snatcher. I'm picking up the boxes — saw them coming loose a few miles back. Be right there. Just wait on me. Over."

Stunned, my mouth hung open as I searched for words. Staring at the CB receiver, I wondered, what on earth had I conjured up? Or better yet, who on earth? But it was too late, I heard the distant blast of a truck horn and saw in my rear-view mirror a semi pulling over, flashing his lights. The Panty Snatcher was on the scene. He approached my vehicle and I got out. "I got a bunch of yer boxes m'am, some look ok..." The Panty Snatcher was cordial, kind and just what I had prayed for, except with a handle that elicited less than pleasant images.

I suppose truckers get a rap as a rather rough bunch even without such appellations. He lashed down my tarp. He said I had too many stored on the roof for safe travel, thus causing the candy exodus. He took the boxes on his truck that I did not need for my first delivery. He would meet me at a truck stop near Tuscaloosa after I had lightened my load in Birmingham at the shops expecting my delivery. The Snatcher had planned to break at this particular truck stop for the evening. This plan would allow me to load the salvaged baskets he had on his truck and take them on with me to visit my daughters at the Tri Delta house.

After a brief stop in Birmingham, I drove to the truck stop somewhere outside Tuscaloosa. At our meeting place, I would recover the wayward goods, such as they were. I called my husband and informed him of my predicament. I told him that if I disappeared, the last place I visited was a truck stop around Tuscaloosa. Poor Jimmy was in disbelief.

I tentatively approached the public address operator

in the truck stop. I straightened up and with as much authority as I could muster, asked him to, "Please tell Night Crawler that Wild Thing is here for her candy baskets." The big, unshaven man in charge of the address system chewed a fried eggroll slowly. He paused, his droopy eyes looked me over, as if he might tell me where to take my request. I pursed my lips, nodded and crossed my arms. He shrugged and made the following announcement.

"Naaght Crawler, Naaght Crawler," He paused and frowned giving me one last check, "Whiiiiald Thang is here for her... Candy baskets. Wild Thing is here for those candy baskets, Night Crawler."

Night Crawler appeared from behind an aisle of beef jerky and fuel injector cleaners. The Panty Snatcher had cleaned up and was in the mood for some dinner. I graciously declined citing the sorority house full of girls waiting on me. This bit of information garnered a raised eyebrow. Maybe that was the wrong excuse considering his moniker. But he turned out to be a perfect gentleman. He helped me reload the wagon with the surviving baskets. He would only accept a few broken baskets as a thank you for his kindness. I delivered the packages and visited my daughters... a few baskets shy but all in all, a successful trip saved by an unlikely hero.

Night Crawler and I kept in touch via CB radio as I made regular delivery trips to Birmingham in the following months. I can say we became friends. I even presented him with a bright plaid, wool shirt at the very truck stop where we had met.

I prayed to the Lord and the Lord answered. He answers in His way and what a wonderful, miraculous way it is.

CHAPTER

WAYLON JENNINGS AND THE GOLD, JEWEL-STUDDED BELT BUCKLE FIASCO

WAYLON'S WIFE JESSI and I became fast friends during the Jennings' sale. I had great respect for them, and grew close to the legendary pair. Waylon was compassionate, in control, and had a sense of humor that would catch me off guard. Jessi and I had much in common and fostered a friendship that lasts to this day.

Maureen, their head assistant, had contacted me to do a sale for them at their home. They were moving from their hilltop manor in Brentwood, putting up a number of his possessions from years of celebrity life. I was asked to help him sell a mountain of items from his home and office.

Waylon's sale began on a bitter cold winter day. There were several hundred people huddled outside, waiting for the doors to open. People had come from all over for a chance to own a piece of history from a living legend of country music. The information cards each guest filled out indicated some had traveled from as far away as Canada.

I placed one of the centerpieces of the sale in a rounded glass case on a piano in a conspicuous location hoping to create some excitement and intrigue. It was one of Waylon's custom, one-of-a-kind gold belt buckles, fashioned with intricate designs and encrusted with jewels. The oversized buckle glimmered and the settings danced with light in the display case. It was to remain in my care until it sold.

I orbited around the sale, returning often to the lustrous buckle as buyers ogled Waylon's personal and professional items. I make it a point to create a path around every sale on which I travel and then retrace my steps. This allows me to keep a watchful eye without appearing to loom over the guests. I had also hired a house full of plain clothes security guards for the event.

The sale was in full swing. Chattering buyers were happily securing treasures. I finished another round working my way back to the case. I stared into the glass. I looked again in disbelief. The case was empty! I felt a deep emptiness in my stomach reflecting the emptiness of the case. Waylon trusted me. I was in charge. What on earth had become of it? I hurried to the phone and called the police.

I then rushed, with arms outstretched, to the heavy wooden doors at the entrance and slammed them shut. Closing with a mighty boom, the room froze and startled eyes turned my way. I latched both doors and turned to face the crowd spreading my arms across the doors for emphasis. I could feel my emotions welling up and my eyes were wild with panic, anger and indignation.

I proclaimed, "Ladies and Gentlemen... there has been a theft. Right here in this room. The doors are locked. The police are on their way, and no one will be allowed to leave until Waylon's belt buckle is recovered." My announcement was caught on camera by a newsman in the crowd. The only thing NOT caught on film was the thief.

Several gasps could be heard from the crowd, as they processed the fact that they were now all part of an investigation. My announcement was met with some resistance and a few of the guests, turned captives, turned suspects, were now clamoring to leave, citing prior engagements. But this was a real life version of the board game Clue. I declare, it must have been Colonel Mustard, with the Candlestick, in the Observatory.

With the sale halted and my staff and security guards strategically positioned at the exit, I made the dreaded call to Waylon to report the disappearance of his ornate accessory. I sought to remain professional, but as I came to the part where I told him it was missing, I was sobbing into the phone over the pilfered buckle.

Waylon was a true Southern gentleman. His deep voice was woven with his calming disposition. Good Southern manners are like peach preserves on well buttered biscuits. "Well Berenice, there must be somebody who wants that buckle a lot more than you or me. I say just let 'em have it. They'll pay the price someday, and Berenice, I guess you better... let my people go." By the end of his words, we were both laughing a little. He sounded like Moses setting Pharaoh straight as I imagine. I dried my eyes as best I could, hoping my makeup wasn't running down my face.

I unlocked the doors and informed the attendees that the sale would have to resume the following morning. The belt buckle was never recovered. Although there was a guest who claimed to have a notion of its whereabouts, the police were unable to ascertain any concrete leads.

Some of the more notable items that we were able to sell were a number of his guitars and antiques. Waylon had a genuine Dukes of Hazard car, which sold for $45,000. We sold a bathrobe of Waylon's on eBay for $375, which I thought was a nice price. But shortly after it sold, I received a call from a woman in Wisconsin who offered a $1000 for the robe. I told her it had already been purchased, and then couldn't help but ask, "Isn't that a bit extravagant?" She cut me short saying, "I can afford anything I want. My birthday is Saturday and I was going to turn on Waylon's music, snuggle up in his robe on the sofa and dream of him all day." I was sorry to turn down such an eager customer, so I contacted Waylon who got a kick out of the story. "Berenice, I have five more robes just like it!" But he didn't send another, so I guess the birthday girl had to find another way to celebrate.

Overall, Waylon and Jessi were pleased with the

outcome of the sale and our work and hired me again some time later to perform a second sale for his office. I was so relieved. It is especially taxing when working with celebrity clients, as their recommendation, or lack thereof, goes a long way with their friends and colleagues. He was not only a great musician and singer, but also a great person.

CHAPTER

In Hong Kong
on Angel Wings

═══════════

I CHOOSE TO LIVE BY TRUSTING. I trust that those I come in contact with will do what they say, and I do my very best to do the same. I feel this gives me an openness that attracts and welcomes others. I see it as part of a Christian life, as part of the Great Commission. How can we "make disciples of all the nations," if we don't engage individuals in a way that creates a receptive heart? *Pass it on!*

Relating to others in a rather unguarded manner can bring stormy skies on occasion. One such circumstance landed me half way around the world. It all began as I was entertaining a new friend, Horace, in my living room. Horace was an interesting individual who had his hand in the international clothing design industry. He came well recommended by a prominent lawyer, who was an assitant district attorney, and my neighbor, the wife of a heart surgeon. Horace and I were beginning to discuss the possibility of developing a business relationship of some sort.

To start, his hook was a fur coat. He had a source and offered to get me a beautiful full-length lunaraine mink for $1500. His idea was that he would even work it out, so I could make a trip to China to pick up the coat. That sounded like great fun to me, so I paid him in advance. The fur coat never made an appearance, and I was out the money, so I held his feet to the fire as far as the trip was concerned. His intricate scheming continued, as he put forth a plan to send me to Hong Kong. I would make some recommendations and consult on pattern decisions with a hot young designer named Karen Lamb, who had worked with Ralph Lauren. Karen's brother lived in Hong Kong, and she was scheduled to go there to make selections on colors, styles and materials for her first line of clothing. For the trip, the idea was, I would be accompanied by Karen Lamb and Darshee, originally from India, whose husband is a Nashville physician. Karen, Darshee and I made plans by phone, but did not meet. It turned out that Darshee was in India and Karen was already in Hong Kong.

Horace had a master plan to import labor from China to America and set up a small working village in South Carolina. He was well connected there, and was going to make the designer wares in his imported Chinese village. I was on board. It sounded fun. I must admit I was flattered that he respected my opinion on fashion enough to send me to China, but oh, for the trappings of the ego. More than once we would make travel arrangements and Horace would say something awful had happened and we had to postpone. His excuses were getting outlandish. Finally, I put my foot down and told him that the next day I was meeting him at the airport. I had planned a trip and announced a trip, and I was going to Hong Kong.

Sure enough, the next day Horace and his travel agent met me at the Nashville airport. I was excited and ready to go. Horace said there was some trouble with my ticket. He said they needed my credit card to pay for the ticket, and he would reimburse me at a later time. I was suspicious and told him my card was maxed out. After getting the runaround so many times, I was fit to be tied, and was not about to give over my card. The uncomfortable situation did not go unnoticed by the airline staff as Horace and I fenced words. He eventually produced a credit card of his own and did at least one thing that he had promised to do.

By the time I was to board, I was so beaten down from the ordeal, I could hardly bring myself to do so, but as I approached the counter, a man from the airline ushered me aside. "I'm gonna do something for you," he said with a smile. "I heard about your troubles with your ticket, and I'm gonna bump you up to first class for your entire flight." I didn't know what to say. I stammered out a "Th... Thank you!?" He grinned, handed me my new seating assignment, taking my old one from my hand, winked and said, "See, every now and then good things can happen in this world." *–Pass It On*

I had seldom flown first class. I eased into the

oversized leather seat with plenty of legroom and felt my fortunes may have changed for the better. I thanked the Lord for this happy occurrence and felt Him ever so near.

The flight was many hours, and I was on board with a number of interesting individuals. The wine and champagne flowed freely, and the delicious food just kept coming. First class was as much party as travel. Over the flight, I conversed with some of the other first classers. Among my new friends were three NBA players and an international jewelry dealer. We talked, laughed and exchanged stories. After dinner, I dug through my purse. Feeling especially effusive, I decided to offer my travel companions a little pill guaranteed by my doctor to help me sleep on the plane. I handed them out like candy mints. I think it was a drug called Halcyon. Anyway, soon the big basketball players were sprawled all over the place, legs and arms splayed everywhere, snoring and completely gone from this world. They evidently had enjoyed even more of the wine than I had. I felt terrible. They had an exhibition game to play and were in no shape for anything but bed. We all slept for the rest of the trip.

The Hong Kong International Airport was buzzing with people and languages from all over the world. I hailed a cab and ended up sharing one with two men from Athens, Greece, who were also staying at the Shangri-La Hotel. On the way, I learned the names of the father and son, Johann and Johannes. They were clothing designers and buyers that traveled the world. They invited me to dinner with them that evening at the hotel. We shared stories of our homelands, and they told me about their latest fashion ideas. We laughed and soaked up the adventure of the exotic setting. They invited me to visit the island of Macau the next day with them to meet some high profile designers for lunch. One was even featured in my tour book as a notable and artistic resident and fashion designer.

Upon my return from Macau, I received a surprise phone call in my hotel room from the jewelry man I had met on the plane. He invited me to attend a big jewelry show with him. While there, I purchased some jewelry with the notion that I could sell it at my shop. Horace had yet to make his appearance, so I decided to make the best possible use of my time.

The next day I called several of the tour agencies informing them that I was there on a tour research mission for my Garden Club back in the U.S. of A. and would like to "sample" their tour choices. Evidently the word got around and I had companies falling over themselves to take me on tours.

Horace's master plan involving the young New York-Hong Kong designer Karen Lamb was still in motion. I was to meet with her and the buyer Darshee who was well connected in the Middle Eastern fabric trade. We eventually found each other, although Horace himself and, I must repeat, the mink coat never showed up. So Karen, Darshee and I endeavored to make the time worthwhile. I viewed the collection and gave advice on what I felt would match Western tastes.

Karen's brother, Peter Lamb, was a children's

clothing designer, and we formed a plan to travel with him into new and remote regions of China searching for and visiting new manufacturing plants. We were told to pack only what we could carry with us, and I kept my room at the Shangri-La. I was off for another turn in the adventure.

We traveled by train into new territories of China. Many of the manufacturing buildings we visited had rickety bamboo scaffolding lacing up their fronts, and we traveled on muddy roads with potholes big enough to get stuck in. I communicated mostly with sign language and had no true itinerary. I sat down on the cutting board in one of the clothes factories when I heard, "Oh, no, no, no. That's bad luck to sit on a cutting board." I quickly removed myself. Funny thing was, I never felt like I was in danger; I was never scared. I had this sense of peace for I knew the Lord was with me. I felt the strength of the passage...

...But they who wait upon the LORD shall renew their strength; they shall mount up with wings as eagles; they shall run, and not be weary; and they shall walk, and not faint. Isaiah 40:31 KJV

One night upon returning to our hotel in China, I noticed strings of Christmas lights decorating the trees in the entryway along with displays of glowing plastic Easter bunnies. It looked as if they were combining two holidays into one. I asked Peter, Karen's brother, what they thought they were celebrating. He laughed and said they were just celebrating to be celebrating and then added, "Ahh, lights, bunnies. It's all the same. We all believe in the same Jesus Christ." Jesus did come for all of us, all customs aside. Still, it seemed like something might have been lost in translation as far as decorations.

That evening in the hotel lobby restaurant and karaoke bar, we cut loose and I ended up on stage singing "My Way" to the hotel guests out on their balconies that overlooked the stage. I even got them chanting, "Hip Hip Hurray for the U.S.A!" and was reluctant to give up the microphone. I suppose the foreign soil emboldened the... ham in me.

It was nearing Easter and Jimmy told me, "Berenice dear, if you don't make it back home by Easter, well, you might as well not bother." I got the message loud and clear, and after my time in China with Peter and extensive work with Karen getting her new line and wardrobe in order, it was time for me to return home, and I did make it in time for Easter.

I returned home just a few weeks before the tragic events of Tiananmen Square transpired. I had no inkling that just underneath the surface boiled such unrest and turmoil. Horace never showed up, yet I managed to have a most memorable trip and met some wonderful people.

I had the pleasure of returning to China in 2011 to visit my granddaughter, Miller Folk, who served as a missionary there. Several members of our family, including grandchildren made the journey with me. It was a powerful experience to meet so many Chinese Christians.

CHAPTER

GROWING UP

———

I WAS FIVE YEARS OLD WHEN the Japanese bombed Pearl Harbor. My father was determined to do his part for the war effort. He joined the military signing up for the Air Force to serve as a doctor during World War II. My dad, Dr. Cleo Miller, was an accomplished physician in Nashville. He had already built the Miller Clinic in 1937, where he combined doctors of various specialties under one roof. His approach to patient care was the first of its kind in Nashville.

Being in the Air Force meant he was stationed all over, and where Dad went, the Miller tribe followed. We drove from base to base all together following each new assignment, two cars full of Millers singing at the top of our lungs. The first car was often composed of Dad, and my brothers Jack and Jimmy, while the second car-load consisted of Mother, my sister Jean Ann (now McNally), our housekeeper Nora and me.

Nora was our much loved African American housekeeper and cook. She traveled wherever we went. We were a big family with lots of moving parts.

Nora kept us well fed and took care of all our needs at home, wherever that was at the time. We children were puzzled by her though. She couldn't eat where we ate, or stay where we stayed. It was hard on her and on us as well. We loved her like a second mother.

My father entered the service as a major and rose to the rank of lieutenant-colonel while at Tyndall Air Base in Panama City, Florida. When Dad received his honors, I was so excited for him that I leaped into his arms and in doing so, caught my arm on his shiny, new Air Force pin and tore a gash which bled profusely and needed stitches, making quite a scene.

Our stay at Tyndall was our longest in one place during our nomadic wartime lifestyle. We were there eighteen months and in the process, Dad became Commander in Chief of the hospital, a position he would subsequently hold at each of the bases to which he was assigned.

We left Tyndall for Columbus Air Force Base for a six month stay and then north to Yale, New Haven Hospital in Connecticut.

We moved into an old three-story house near New Haven. I remember a hurricane coming in, nearly tearing the old house apart. I still remember how frightened we were. The wind and rain roared for what seemed like forever, shaking the old structure and us in it.

Dad took care of everything through that storm and many others. He was not only our father, but also the family doctor as well. I recall brother Jimmy's appendix rupturing. Dad had sterilized instruments with him at all times and proceeded right then and there to remove Jimmy's appendix. The power went out during the surgery, and Dad finished the operation by flashlight. He was known for his adept incision-making ability, leaving a minute scar, and was known to complete an appendectomy in less than five minutes.

At the time, the common procedure for post-operative care was a long period of bed rest, during which muscles would atrophy and many patients would grow ever weaker. This made recovery an arduous and lengthy process. Dad began to train his medical personnel to get wounded soldiers back on their feet quickly. This innovation resulted in stronger men in less time. He was a pioneer in the practice of post surgical early ambulation, a practice embraced today across medical fields.

The Miller family next packed up and headed to Scott Air Force Base in Bellville, Illinois. My southern accent stood in stark contrast to the nasal speaking northerners. Every morning I had to be up at 5:00 to catch the bus, which I dreaded. I was mocked for my accent. They even called me a "hillbilly." This teasing hurt me, and I felt like a foreigner in my own country. This move was not a happy time. Thankfully, it was a fairly short assignment and we again set off, this time to Boca Raton Air Force Base in Florida.

Road trips were a choral event for our family. Dad loved to sing and Mom chimed in. We would sing songs like "Mandy Lee," "Grandfather's Clock," "Old

Rugged Cross," and "I Love You Truly," as we traveled. Dad entertained us the whole way, singing, telling jokes and funny stories. Later, we actually performed as the "Miller Quintet." We sang all the old favorites, and Dad played guitar at the Lion's Club, churches and any place that would have us.

Papa, Dad's father, came to live with us in Boca Raton. I followed in Dad's footsteps playing practical jokes on Papa. Once, I aimed the garden hose through an open window as he reclined in a nearby easy chair and exclaimed, "Papa, Papa it's raining!" He came after me shaking his cane in the air, mostly in jest I am sure, but I did get him soaked.

My father's brother, Elmore Hill was a huge practical joker in his own right. My Dad and Elmore, beloved Nashville oral surgeon, were very close. They conspired to prank most everyone. Elmore credited Dad as mentor and benefactor while making his way through dental school, and he was one of my most loved uncles.

In 1945, the war came to an end and the Miller clan returned to Nashville. We were happy to be able to go home, but on our return, we were met by a disheartening discovery. Our English Tudor house, our lovely home in a beautiful setting, was in disrepair. It was on the site of the old Inglewood Country Club and had been designed by noted architect Edwin Keeble. We had rented out the house in our absence, and it had not been well cared for. My mother's flower gardens were overgrown and unrecognizable.

Dad had built the first clay tennis court in Nashville, and that too had deteriorated. I recall happily helping him line the court for matches. We all played, and I took to the sport.

Ed.'s note: Berenice was NIL champ in high school. (The NIL was the forerunner of the TSSAA.) Daughter Kathy Denton Stumb was TSSAA state champ, and granddaughter Carlee Petro is state champion on the Mountain Brook High School tennis team in Birmingham, Alabama. Four generations of tennis players sprung from that clay court.

We moved across town to Belle Meade Boulevard in order for the property to be restored to its pre-war condition. Yet, we never returned to the old East Nashville Tudor home, which is still there and listed on the National Register.

Dad returned to his practice after the war, and went from being an old-fashioned family doctor to specializing in surgery. He still made time to take care of families and their medical needs. He made house calls following a full day of work. He would perform a surgery at 6:00 in the morning and then see 100 patients in a day. His stamina and energy seemed endless. I would go with him on his evening house calls, as often as I could. I had the job of shining a big car spotlight on the house numbers to find the address of his patient. Dad called me "Peg" from the song "Peg o' My Heart". I inherited his zeal for work and life. It was all those nights being his little assistant that instilled in me a work ethic that has aided me in my professional life over the years.

When I was very young, I almost died of an empyema, an unusual abscess near my lung. Dad took care of me though, and I fought to live. This alliance against illness gave us a special bond that I felt my entire life growing up.

Dad was also doctor to the stars of the Grand Ole Opry and befriended a number of the sometimes wild bunch. Hank Williams was one of particular note. On one occasion when Hank had been indulging or perhaps over indulging in the vices he was accustomed to, he called on my Dad. When he returned, Dad said, "I think I just heard the next best seller. Hank calls it "Jambalaya and Crawfish Pie and File Gumbo." Because Dad played guitar as well, it has been thought that he and Hank had a jam session after his medical exam.

Roy Acuff was another of the glittering patients Dad cared for. I remember going to the Opry and Roy spotlighting us in the crowd, introducing Dad, and speaking of him as a trusted friend. Dad even traveled to Russia with Acuff on tour at one time.

My Mother, Kathryn Cotton Miller was a Southern Belle, friend to all, and loving mother. She devoted countless hours to Westminster Presbyterian Church as a volunteer. She was known as the "meeter and greeter" there and took her role quite seriously. Her warm welcoming ways made her friends wherever she went. Mom and son Jack's wife, Ann Riley Miller were some of the founders of the Westminster School, a special school for children with learning differences. This school has grown into what is now the Currey Ingram Academy in Brentwood.

Brother Jimmy was once co-owner of Goo Goo Candy, Jack, an orthopedic surgeon, and sister Jean Ann McNally, a healing minister and preacher.

I attended Vanderbilt University and pledged Pi Beta Phi sorority. There I met the love of my life, James (Jimmy) Denton. We had one date as freshmen and then we migrated into the realm of friendship over the next three years. In our senior year, we shared several classes together. It was my good fortune to have the books for one of our classes and Jimmy did not. So he and I studied together frequently. Our love bloomed and we were "pinned" by the end of our senior year.

After graduation, my parents sent me on a trip to Europe as a graduation present. I went with a chaperoned group of about thirty friends. For six weeks we traveled all over Europe. As we traveled, antiques caught my eye everywhere. My degree in Fine Arts all of a sudden became very relevant, and I felt things falling into place. The realization led me to appreciate and purchase some special items to bring home, much to my mother's delight. So began my love of antiques.

Upon my arrival at the Nashville airport, I saw an anxious looking Jimmy waiting for me. He was the only person I wanted to see when I got off the plane. I had missed him so much. He asked me to marry him right there, pulling out a sparkling engagement ring. Jimmy made an early departure from the Marines after tearing up his knee. We were married the following Christmas. We made our home in "Stork Hollow," a fondly coined name for the area where a number of young couples, who had been friends at Vanderbilt, set up housekeeping and started families. Before long I was a mom, and we were a full family, running all over Nashville with babies and children's activities. Jimmy and I have four wonderful children, Debbie, Kathy, Julie and Jim.

Debbie is married to Michael Folk, and they live in Memphis. They were babies together in our duplex in Stork Hollow and reconnected at the University of Alabama. Their children are Catherine, Miller, Michael and Lizzie.

Kathy lives in Nashville with husband Tom Stumb. Their children are Tee, Gracie, Mary Denton, Katy and Jake.

Daughter Julie and her husband Mark Petro live in Birmingham. Their daughters are Carlee and Allee.

Jim lives in Memphis with his wife Liesl and their young children Leelee and Jamie.

CHAPTER

5

A Not So Smooth
Visit To My Son
at College

======

JIM WAS THE LAST of our four children. Living with three older sisters guaranteed him plenty of attention. He grew up spoiled and strong willed, often being exasperated by my haphazard ways. I suppose most children do the same to some extent, but I seemed to keep my son flushed with embarrassment for most of his teenage years.

When son Jim was in school at SMU in Dallas, my heartstrings were pulled in his direction on a regular basis. I made every effort to visit him as often as I could to check on him. So it was on one such trip, that Jim invited me to attend an evening class with him. The class had something to do with films; I figured that sounded most interesting.

I searched in vain for a parking space on campus, I was late and getting anxious. "Ah there's one, no. Ah here's one, oh, No Parking!" I swerved up and down the maze of campus side streets, as the students walked to and fro, toting heavy backpacks; they looked like sherpas searching for Mt. Everest. They kept an eye on me at the cross walks. "Oh, Jim, Mom's gonna miss your class!"

It was dusk and hard to see. I scoured the car-lined streets and started to consider pulling up on the grass. Just then, I noticed an electronic arm rise at the exit of a campus parking lot. In a flash of compulsion, I punched the gas and swerved into the parking lot exit. I thought I could slide in before the exiting car made its escape. Whump-Pssssssst! My rental car lurched forward over something tall and resistant, making a terrible sound. I failed to heed the violent signal and after a momentary pause, I mashed the gas a second time. Whump-Psssssst! This time my head nearly hit the roof of the car as the engine roared, and I watched a puff of smoke rise from beneath my struggling vehicle.

I looked up at a woman waiting to exit. She sat gripping her steering wheel with her mouth wide open and eyebrows raised. Our eyes met and she shook her head and slowly mouthed the most disheartening words, "F-L-A-T T-I-R-E" thus verifying my now growing fear; I was definitely going to miss Jim's class.

I jumped out of my car and found that I had flattened, not one, but all four tires; the one-way spikes had been hidden from me in the late light of the day. My car looked like a whale tossed unceremoniously upon a beach. It sat on the rims, low to the ground looking sad. A line of cars formed, all hopelessly attempting to exit. My car now sat dead in the water, blocking their egress.

Car door flung open, I could see angry faces looking my way. I took a step back, waved and said, "Well, grab a book!" I ran toward the rotunda to seek help. I frantically asked passers by, "Do you know Jim Denton?" I pushed open classroom doors, asking for help. "Do you know Jim Denton?" In room after room, the startled professors and stunned students looked back blankly. After a string of failures, a professor did more than look back with disdain and offered to let me use his office phone. I dialed AAA and thanked the professor for his kindness and apologized for disrupting his class. He seemed to find the entire thing quite amusing. I finally found someone who knew Jim. He took me to his class on the third floor, where I found out he had left to look for me thirty minutes earlier.

By now my car had drawn a curious, mad crowd. I returned to the scene to meet the tow truck man. His name was Charlie. It was embroidered in red cursive on his blue shirt. Charlie exclaimed, "Ehh, you got four flats! Four flat tires! I can't do anything with this. I'm gonna need a flatbed." Charlie's big, stubbled face contorted into a grimace and grew deep shades of purple. As he turned in a mighty huff to leave, I was determined to stand my ground. "Oh and Charlie, when you return, I hope you bring back a better attitude." I cut my eyes and smiled, to drive home my point. I was in no mood to be lectured by the very company I paid to save me from such circumstances, even if they were occasionally self-inflicted. To Charlie's credit, he returned with a much sunnier disposition.

My son arrived. He was embarrassed and in disbelief. My flattened rental was loaded onto the truck and, thanks to the recommendation of my new professor friend, went on its way to a reputable shop. The rental company insisted I was on the hook to replace all four tires. I was so thankful for the help of the professor, I offered to take him to dinner. Jim was fairly bent out of shape over the entire event and said he had a big test the next day and could not accompany us to dinner.

The professor was a suspiciously dapper African-American who felt free to share with me his sexual escapades in some detail, too much detail. He insisted I come to his apartment and see his furniture. I was uneasy. I didn't know what kind of nut job he might be, so I popped in the door and pointed wildly and said, "That's good, that's good and that's good. Now we've got to go eat!" He took me to the finest restaurant. It was a hot spot right off campus; I turned my rings over so no one would talk. Then I had to pay for the whole thing. I should have known something was up when Jim said he had to study for a test. He was well known on campus, but not for his love of academics.

The next day I flew home, but before departing I paid a visit to the president of the university. I told him I thought the spikes were just awful and certainly an over-aggressive measure to protect their precious parking. I asked, "Has anyone else ever done such a thing?"

He said, "Well, yes, once some visiting Chinese professors did, but they only blew out two tires."

Don't pass it on!

CHAPTER

OPPOSITION IN OHIO

<hr>

THIS PARTICULAR SALE requires a bit of background information to appreciate what a tenuous situation it was. A wealthy doctor had passed on. He had a domestic partner whom he had been with for many years. They had acquired a small fortune in art and antiques. His partner's health was failing, and he had been in assisted living for some time, blind and with both legs removed below the knees due to diabetes. In his absence, the doctor had been befriended for three weeks before his death by a man whose motives were less than honorable. The doctor had a grown daughter who was to be the executor of his estate, until she was replaced by the mean, self-serving man who had "befriended" her father.

The situation became a court case and, of course, went before a judge. Parties included the doctor's daughter, the blind partner's niece, who was her uncle's executor, and the man who was newly named as the doctor's executor. The word was, that the new executor had stolen several priceless items from the house in the interim. Of note, a Picasso painting and an extensive silver collection ($175,000) went missing before the locks could be changed. The niece of the doctor's blind partner knew me, and recommended to the judge that I handle the estate sale. This notion was met with great resistance from the mean man who thought he was the new executor, and who had one of his cronies in mind for the job for a further fleecing of the deceased. The judge saw fit to appoint me to be in charge of the entire estate sale, wading through injunction after injunction thrown at me from the new executor.

The original executor, the daughter of the prominent doctor, had warned me that the sale was not without drama and trouble. The new executor seemed out to get me from the word go.

I knew I was in for a wild ride once I arrived at the 13,000 square foot mansion, named Runnymede. The home was filled with old paintings and tapestries from all over the world along with collections of English, French and American antique furniture. The sad thing was how far the interior of the house had deteriorated. The home had not been cleaned in some two years and was an absolute mess. The two had been known to throw wild, lavish parties. It appeared as though no one had hung around to clean up from the last one. We fell to cleaning, pricing and setting up for the sale, that I was determined to make happen!

The new executor was roiled by my being named to do the sale. He petitioned the judge claiming I could not carry out a sale in a foreign state. The judge dismissed this foolishness, as my license is good in all states. My expertise was challenged. I felt like I was making a real enemy, and all I sought to do was my job, which was difficult enough with the house in such a state. The newly named executor and his lawyer showed up at the house three days before the sale began, as he was obligated by order of the judge to preview the sale. They lurked around with rotten dispositions glaring at my staff.

Two of my granddaughters, Katy and Mary Denton Stumb had come to help me do the sale. They were told to be my eyes and ears while the two "bad guys" poked around leering at everybody. The younger one peered at him from a long hallway leading to the parlor where he loitered. He bent over and picked up a silver pocket watch, thinking he was alone. Then my little granddaughter, Katy, let him have it. "Put that down," she said, delivering the message with all the force a third grader could muster. Startled, he looked incredulous, set the pocket watch down, and stormed out.

Katy set up a lemonade stand during the sale keeping her earnings in a small velvet bag. In time, with the sale's theme of trouble, her moneybag was stolen. She was crushed. The neighbors gathered funds together and during the sale, presented her with replacement money that amounted to much more than her sales. She was so grateful. We all were. The neighbors quickly became friends, even having us over for dinner and lunch. I even hired a few of them to help me out.

The sale was such a large event that several zealous customers literally camped out in the yard. The doors opened at 7:00 a.m. and the crowd poured in. I made it through. Sometimes that's all you can hope for in this business. I made loads of new friends in Dayton, Ohio and still keep in touch with a number of them. This was one of the largest sales I have ever done. People came from all over the state and as far away as New York. Also, several faithful customers traveled from Nashville.

CHAPTER

MILLSTONE MELEE

―――――

THE SPRING AIR was sweet with the smell of honeysuckle and fresh cut grass. The blue sky looked like water warm enough to jump in. The tat-tat-tats of the mowers that hum every weekend in the warm months were in full undulating chorus. I wound through the country roads just outside downtown Franklin, a small town south of Nashville, on my way to a sale.

I arrived at the farm where the sale was to be held, prior to the owner's move from the old farmhouse. I walked around the man's yard with him, admiring the property, when I noticed a massive millstone poking out of the ground near his front door. The partially buried millstone obviously looked as if it had been there a long time, and he seemed unaware that it was anything special.

Millstones are highly sought after decorative pieces. In their original capacity they were used in gristmills to grind grains into flour, and into animal feed.

Hewn from burrstone, sandstone or limestone, some were banded with metal rings. In France, the patterns chiseled into some of the very old millstones were patented, as the designs were often artistic expressions significant to the particular farm.

"If I dig it up, can I buy it from you?" I asked

The farmer laughed, "Honey, if you dig that thing up, you can have it."

"Then have it… I shall!" I thought. I felt a challenge coming on, but I was without tools and the stone looked as if it weighed many hundreds of pounds. I am usually reticent to become a buyer at my own sales, but this was just too good to pass up. The sale began, and I began my dig. I grabbed a large spoon from the collection to be sold and headed back outside and started digging. Thus putting myself in a most unflattering position, bent over, unceremoniously jabbing at the dirt and grass that held my prize captive. After some time, the farmer took pity on me and brought me a shovel, shaking his head at my persistence (or craziness). This ninety-year-old man got a real kick out of my efforts. I refused to let him or anyone help me. "I am diggin' my gravestone." I said.

All my activity drew a crowd of neighbors and they all had opinions as to how I might get home with my millstone. My idea was to place it in the back of my van. This notion was met with skepticism and even some laughter. I was informed that the millstone weighed over three hundred pounds and would most certainly flatten my tires.

One of the curious neighbors, in the crowd of onlookers, stepped forward and volunteered. He came to my aid with his bobcat tractor and a flatbed trailer. With the help of many; the millstone was loaded up in proper fashion. The farmer decided he wanted $250 once it became apparent that I really was going to extract the artifact from his yard. The neighbor farmer delivered it to my home that evening, stopping traffic on my street and causing loads of curiosity. I was also on the hook to fix the yard where my excavation had left a huge hole. Eighteen bags of dirt, ten bales of hay and three bags of grass seed later, our deal was done. By the time it was all over, it had cost me an arm and a leg, but I have a piece of art and history in my front yard.

I joked that while I was digging with that spoon, I wondered if I was digging up my own tombstone. It very well could have been, but with an intrepid spirit, plenty of grace and help from others, much is possible. The stone stands on my front lawn as a formidable trophy for my efforts. Every now and then a passer-by stops and tries to buy it from us, but so far, no one has offered enough to curb my fondness of it. Not one of our children has yet to ask me to *pass it on*.

All David had was a slingshot and five smooth stones against a giant. All I had was a spoon and an idea against a three hundred pound stone.

CHAPTER

CHEFS, CHEFS
&
MORE CHEFS

―――――

I WAS WORKING AN ESTATE sale on Page Road, in Nashville, one cold, rain-filled day. A woman walked in, whom I knew represented owners of a number of dilapidated properties on and around Murphy Road. She asked if I was interested in looking at a piece of property in that area. I sensed a great possibility. It had been a long-time dream of mine to own a restaurant with shops. This location seemed like it might just be the fit for a one-stop-shopping venue. The realtor drove me over to the site, and what a sight it was. Two houses sat slumped against one another, as if they were tired of standing. One was falling down on the backside and the walls appeared to be kicked in, but I saw potential, and with the owner under time pressure to make a deal, I felt the situation was ripe for negotiation. We arranged to meet with the property owner to hash out a deal.

The seller wore a long black overcoat, black boots, a tall black hat, and had a long wispy white beard that made him look like a character from a Dickens novel. He seemed to have stepped out of another time. Perhaps I should have taken his peculiar appearance as a sign of things to come.

I strode headlong, despite such a clue, dragging Jimmy and our son Jim to see the disheveled mess. Then, against their advice, I made an offer on the property, and it was accepted. The codes department informed me that I would need to hire a contractor if repairs would exceed $25,000. I was sure they would not, and I was determined, yet inexperienced, to be my own contractor. However, once the dust had settled, the "repairs" cost many times that sum.

Over the coming weeks and months the ramshackle buildings began to take shape. The garage was transformed into a floral shop and office. We fixed the roofs, joining the structures together, which no one thought could be done, and opened a beauty salon in the upstairs. We opened a gift shop and a restaurant in the now-conjoined buildings. I named the restaurant after my husband, calling it Yogi's. My husband was given the nickname Yogi by our oldest granddaughter Catherine Folk, and it has stuck with him ever since. She thought he looked like Yogi Bear. Naming the restaurant after him was partially an honor and partially a joke; he was so against going into the restaurant business. As a banker, he was loath to make loans to anyone aspiring to be a restaurateur. Yet Yogi's was open, and we were in the restaurant business.

My new venture cost me a great deal of sleep and a fair share of worry. I continued to add to the dream, and to the cost. We added a glassed-in porch and later, a tented area in the back, complete with an ornate, three-tiered fountain, increasing our capacity to over sixty guests. We regularly hosted bridal parties, luncheons and joy-filled dinner parties. My longtime vision of creating a place to serve multiple needs of customers was coming to fruition.

The dream was not without its fair share of perplexities though. We built a bridge over the creek connecting to a landscape company in the back to access more parking. I was contacted by the Metro Codes department and informed that they had received complaints from neighbors concerned that my bridge might encourage open-air copulation. They were worried people would be enticed to have sex beneath our bridge. I was dumbfounded and ignored the absurd complaint.

This, however, was not the only incident that put my ability to "love thy neighbor" to the test. One man who lived nearby, when cars were parked on the street in front of his house, would park so close to our customers' cars, they couldn't get out. He would then stand at his glass front door in his birthday suit, as a surprise on their return, much to the embarrassment and shock of my poor guests.

Nails were propped under employees' and guests' tires by the owner of the wishy washy place next door. Some of my customers were even shouted at. It seemed we were far from welcome by some who lived in the area.

My next big challenge was hiring a true chef. I had cooks, but I wanted someone who would manage the kitchen in a professional manner and generally take good care of things in my absence. I hired a chef from Mexico, who promptly threw a raucous Cinco de Mayo party at Yogi's complete with a mariachi band. He invited all his closest family and friends, of which there seemed to be an endless supply. Yogi's was packed with rollicking Mexicans and the entire party was on me. Our fiesta-throwing chef was relieved of his duties shortly thereafter.

My next hire came from Puerto Rico. He cordially invited Jimmy and me to a New Year's Eve party. We happily accepted, seeking to form good relations with our new chef. Unbeknownst to us, he ordered six turkeys with all the trimmings and charged them to the restaurant. We were underwriting his soirée in high fashion. I was able to halt this train before it left the station. The kind man, who owned the service station across the street, called me at six o'clock one morning, informing me of some strange goings-on at my restaurant. When I arrived, I found the chef's van loaded down with turkeys, cakes, pies and countless bags of dry foodstuffs. I crept into the shop next door and overheard him talking with someone. This outrageous chef was planning to set me up and have his lawyer sue me! All the nefarious details I will never know. I appeared in the doorway, much to their surprise, and informed the chef and waiter I had overheard the entire plan. Amazingly he stuck around, likely hoping I would fire him so he might draw unemployment. I cut his hours back to a bare minimum until one day he disappeared. The running score was 0 for 2 in the chef department.

The next chef I hired was a hard working woman. I was taken by her work ethic and incredibly long hours. Coming in early and staying late, she told me she just loved her job. It was some time before I realized that she was living under her desk at the restaurant. Sadly, we could not keep her on as both employee and phantom tenant. That was 0 for 3.

Our next chef turned out to be a raging alcoholic. She ran off with the electrician, shortly after being hired. One chef went off on his bike for his lunch break but did not return. I received a call from the police informing me that he had been arrested in a drug deal. So much for chefs four and five.

I had two caterers as chefs. Unbeknownst to me, I was funding their catering businesses. I guess they figured I was not paying attention and maybe I wasn't. Eventually, I did notice stacked up trays of food in my kitchen and cooler, along with a single order for 75 loaves of bread. Not that you're counting, but that's failed chefs six and seven. I found it quite difficult to be an absentee owner.

After a fifteen-year journey, we decided to lease the space to Willie Thomas, former head chef at Capitol Grille, where he opened the eclectic Park Café that has long stood as a Nashville favorite for locals in the know. I sold the building to him. My family admitted that I might have a little savvy, after all.

I learned one lesson: Never be an absentee owner of a restaurant.

Incidentally, I found I couldn't stay away from the

restaurant business and currently own the Cottage Cafe in Bellevue. I can honestly say that I now have the best team of all. Lorie and Jason have done wonders.

Evidentially, not being able to stay away is a running theme, I also opened a gift shop and consignment shop – both connected to the Cottage Cafe, located at 162 Belle Forest Cir. Some opportunities I just can't seem to *pass on*.

CHAPTER

9

A Bear Encounter

I NEARLY KILLED BEAR BRYANT

YEARS AGO, MY daughter Kathy Stumb was on the University of Alabama tennis team. I made it a custom to leave Goo Goo candy clusters as a little present with the coaching staff when I visited. The tennis courts were right next to the football field, and all the athletic offices were together. I would visit with the tennis coaches, and I happened to know Coach Bailey, who was one of Bear Bryant's assistant coaches.

One day I was going up the stairs to the athletic offices, not paying particular attention to anyone coming down those same stairs. I did notice someone passing by and said, "Oh, Coach Bailey," thinking it was my friend. The surprised man looked at me with wide eyes, and said, "I am Paul Bear Bryant." He was polite, but I could tell I had made a huge blunder. Here was "The Bear" in his own building being mistaken for one of his assistants. I apologized saying, "I didn't recognize you without your hat!" I continued chatting on about my daughter playing tennis there. I finally got a smile when I mentioned that I was the lady who always left the Goo Goos for him.

On that same trip, I had brought my two girls a suede jacket to share as a gift. I had packed it in my suitcase and planned to surprise them once I arrived. My dog Coco had suspected I was leaving her, and in a fit of anger took some hamburger meat discarded in the trash and buried it among the clothes in my unzipped suitcase before I left home. I made it to my girls' sorority house and unzipped my suitcase to take out the suede jacket only to be met by an incredible odor. The whole house suddenly smelled like a dead animal. I was persona non grata for a while there.

A few months later I was on a plane heading out of Birmingham. The Bear happened to be on the same flight. I had some Goo Goos with me and decided it was a good chance to smooth things over since our last awkward encounter. I gave the candies to the flight attendant and asked her to give them to The Bear "from the Goo Goo lady." A short while later there was a commotion near the front of the plane, and people were jumping up and coughing could be heard.

I later asked the flight attendant what had happened. She replied, "The Bear nearly choked on those candies you had me give him!" She made a face at me and stormed off. Well, so much for smoothing things over with the Bear. Some things you don't want to *"pass on."*

CHAPTER

10

SOMETHING STRANGE
IN THE
SANTA FE HILLS

═══════

THE JANUARY SUN nestled itself in between the sandy, scrub brush covered hills. Contorted silhouettes of desert trees stood upon the horizon as the elongated shadows whipped by. I stared out the back passenger window of our taxi. My sister Jean Ann McNally and I, along with Lynn Baker, a Nashville decorator, were in route from the Albuquerque airport to conduct a sale at a Victorian mansion in the old part of town.

Sad circumstances surrounded the sale, as our client's wife had died unexpectedly of pneumonia on Christmas day, no more than a month before. The couple was building a retreat in the Santa Fe Hills that would double as a bed and breakfast. The sale of possessions and home would be part of their transition to their new lifestyle.

The Victorian mansion was full of antiques she had collected over the years. It looked like a Walt Disney house complete with a spiral staircase in a round turret and a long porch decorated with requisite Victorian gingerbread. There was not much yard, as it sat on a prominent corner lot bordered by a white picket fence. The mid Victorian home and furnishings stood in contrast to the local southwestern style.

I had been there earlier to visit and do the pricing, so we got down to the business of preparing for the sale. With pricing done, I could focus on advertising the event. I called on the local antique shops, put up flyers and sent out invitations to the surrounding area. We hoped to spur interest by spreading the word far and wide. The Internet was just catching on, and I even placed ads electronically.

Our efforts to advertise the sale seemed to be effective. The night before opening, several people were literally camped outside the manor waiting for the doors to open. We were nearly overrun by customers eager to look and buy. At one point of particular chaos, both Jean Ann and Lynn sold a large piece of furniture to two different customers. When the second customer returned to pick up their purchase, Lynn exited stage right (to the restroom) in a hurry. I knew he was avoiding the scene, and I grabbed at his ponytail trying to reel him back in, but he was too quick for me. I was left to apologize and face the angry customer and return her money.

After two days of selling in the old-town mansion. Jean Ann, Lynn and I were invited to the hills of

Santa Fe to have dinner with our client in his other, newly constructed home. It was a massive hacienda. The adobe architecture spilled out over the hill in every direction. Our gracious host toured us around the austere structure pointing out the most impressive things about the construction. Everything was large, oversized and seemed to have a man's touch to it. This was definitely his place. He told us that he planned to continue on with opening his bed and breakfast and seemed uninterested in talking about his late wife or even about the sale. After the tour, he retired briefly and left us to relax on a terrace and enjoy the views over cocktails until it was time for dinner.

We were shown to a large dining room where we were seated at a long, dark wooden table. The room was lit by candles, and our host was yet to appear. His "help" said he would be right down. He entered the room in an animated fashion, calling for wine to be brought to the table. He said, "We have another guest joining us this evening for dinner." He flashed an impish grin and continued, "My new neighbor, Isabella will be over shortly. She has been a great help to me in the last month." Almost on cue, Isabella appeared in the doorway, young, beautiful and buxom. Her deep brown hair and tanned skin contrasted with her white southwestern dress. He stood to greet her with an embrace. Lynn had given us a little "heads up" about the situation.

Jean Ann was making eyes at me and biting her lip. I did all I could to keep a sunny disposition and show no signs of surprise. As the fine dinner of authentic Mexican cuisine progressed, I tried to talk about the ongoing sale, which to me was of great interest, but he repeatedly changed the subject. He did the same thing when I spoke of his recently deceased wife.

Isabella took charge as soon as she arrived. She said she had recently purchased and moved into a ranch just down the road. She inserted herself even into his plans, stumbling out we's instead of I's when telling stories. Jean Ann, Lynn and I made as quick an exit as we could after dinner. As we were leaving to return to his Victorian home, our host raised his wine glass, looked me dead in the eye and said, "Sell everything. Sell it down to the walls and floors." We had our marching orders, albeit under dubious circumstances.

The truth is we had heard rumors that there might be another woman hanging around. The circumstances of his late wife's passing were reportedly strange. Her pneumonia may have been left partially untreated until it was too late. By the time I lay my head on the pillow, I had contrived an entire nefarious plot I thought had taken place. It was all circumstantial, but with so many glaring innuendos, how could I not wonder?

For the following two days we continued the sale, and it was an overwhelming success. The lady of the house had been a collector of fine and rather peculiar clothes. Jean Ann, Lynn and I decided to dress for the occasion in some of the more eccentric wares, but piece-by-piece, those were sold as well. We sold some odd things, like an old coke machine and even an antique pump organ. The sale was flooded with the townspeople, as it seemed an estate sale was a novelty there. I think many were just curious as to what was in the stately Victorian mansion in Albuquerque, like a three-piece suit at a pool party. As instructed, we sold everything; right down to the beds we slept in and the towels we used that morning.

It seemed the owner was free to begin again. The couple had no children, and now most everything from his former life had been sold. As for the details of the events leading up to his new life...well, we were just the hired help, and who on earth was I to speculate or cast aspersions?

CHAPTER

11

A Wolf, Cicadas, Snakes and a Slew of Misadventures

M'am, You Need Pants!

MOST OF THE TIME, my sales go smoothly, without hilarity and with nothing out of the ordinary whatsoever. I wouldn't want to come across as someone who invites chaos or, Heaven forbid, trouble. Well, there was the time I enlisted Jimmy to help me. My staff couldn't make it in due to a snowstorm that hit Nashville. I had two sales that day, so I headed to one and Jimmy the other.

He knocked on the door in the quiet, upscale neighborhood in Green Hills. The door opened and there stood the lady of the house, an attractive blonde. She stood there in her bathrobe, which was hanging open in a most revealing way. That robe was all she had on! Jimmy said he, "just sort of looked away," and told her he thought it would be a good idea for her to get some clothes on, as the sale would be starting shortly. Jimmy peered into the house and to his surprise he saw a veritable menagerie; a cockatiel, two cats, a goat, a ferret, a poodle and a real, live blue-eyed wolf. Each day of the sale the homeowner would retreat to her bedroom and come out a totally different person. She seemed a little loopy, and I suspected she was disappearing in order to sneak a drink. She may very well have been an alcoholic, which would certainly help explain her lack of modesty.

Somehow Jimmy made it through what must have been an embarrassing morning; not to mention the presence of a predator in the house, two if you count the wolf. He has never volunteered to help with a sale since; I suppose once bitten twice shy.

BERENICE'S BAIT SHOP

Then there was the time we held a sale in Lewisburg, Tennessee at a lakeside home. The owner was an avid fisher-woman who had a secret bait that evidently did the job. The secret was out when we found 45 jars of cicadas in the freezer. Those noisy bugs emerge in droves, and when they do, we're all sweeping them off our porches as they near pestilence levels for a few weeks. The batch of these little critters can be on a seven or thirteen-year cycle. They are present in Nashville, eating bark and leaves, making a racket as I write. Their mating call is a loud, shrill buzzing that continuously hums in the trees. It is hard to imagine if you have not experienced a cicada invasion.

I decided to try and sell the frozen cicadas and priced them at $3 a jar. I sold them all and probably could have charged $5 from the reaction of folks. One customer asked, "When I thaw them out, will they come back to life?" "I have no idea! Take 'em home and try." I replied. Several buyers also asked for fishing rights at the private lake. I agreed to let them fish there until the house was sold.

And To My Cats I Leave...

One client of mine left his entire fortune, over $600,000, to his three cats. He requested his niece be their caretaker. He left nothing to the rest of his flabbergasted relatives. The cats were old, all in their late teens (in people years). His niece seemed to have a good sense of humor about the whole thing. She said, "I'm gonna build the biggest cathouse in Nashville, because they're not gonna last much longer." The remainder of the inheritance was to go to the Humane Shelter after the last cat's death. She was going to have to get creative while they were still breathing.

THE UNINVITED SNAKE

On another occasion I was holding a sale at a palatial
Italian villa that sat on a hilltop off Hillsboro Road.
I was met at the door by the homeowner who
cautioned me that a copperhead had been killed in
the expansive foyer the night before. I stood in the
huge marble entry hall lined with boxes upon boxes.
I imagined one of my staff or, Heaven forbid, a
customer rummaging through a box and coming
across one of those aggressive and venomous
serpents. "This just won't do," I thought. So I donned
a pair of heavy leather work gloves and checked
every box. I am terrified of snakes, but the thought
of having to inform my staff of the possibility of a
snake slithering out of our inventory gave me cause
enough to face the fear. I thank God that I did not
find any of the snake's friends and was able to carry
on snake free for the entire sale.

A PRECIOUS PIANO

There was a beautiful antique piano included in a
sale at the home of a woman who was in the country
music industry. Our client was reluctant to part with
it, as it was a prized possession. Mary Denton
Stumb, my then five-year-old granddaughter, was
"helping out" and was drawn toward the piano like a
moth to light. She sat down to play on it, banging on
the ivories in a most rambunctious way. This threw
the rather uptight woman into a fit. She exclaimed,
"Oh my piano, my beautiful fine piano! No one is

allowed to play this piano." She pointed dramatically, and my granddaughter froze for just a moment. Mary Denton then composed herself, slipped off the bench, looked up, smoothed her dress and remarked, "I was just thinking about buying it."

VW SOFA

A couple at one sale bought a seven-foot sofa. Not unusual, but what ensued after their purchase certainly borders on the unusual. They had driven a tiny VW to the sale and were determined to take the oversized sofa home. After much wrangling, the couple pulled away with the sofa tied to the top and only the tires showing.

Jo Gourley, whom I called Baba, sold them that sofa. She was a dear friend and such a saleswomen. She knew how to create a vision for the customer, and her charm and grace did the rest.

SELLING IT ALL

A family from England came to one of our sales located on Ensworth Avenue near the school. It turned out they were purchasing the house across the street. They started looking around and pointing to all the items they liked and wanted. They decided to buy out the entire sale on the spot the morning the sale opened. We put up our Sold Out sign and all went home.

I have had cause to sell it even further than down to the floorboards and windows. In fact, I sold the windows, the staircase, the fixtures and the bricks in a sale in Monterey, Tennessee. I had a time deciding what to charge for bricks. On another occasion, I "sold the house out" for a District Attorney whose home was in Belle Meade. We even sold the hardware for him. It was amazing to see both houses taken apart piece by piece. Now this was serious repurposing!

Another clean sweep happened at a sale in Leiper's Fork, a lovely little community south of Nashville. The house was enormous, 22,000 square feet, and owned by a country music icon. A number of fine items were to be sold. We had held a private sale one week before our public sale. The private sale was by invitation only and consisted of friends and regular clients.

The day before the public sale, a couple from Calhoun, Georgia bought everything in the house directly from the owner. I was informed that the sale was to be cancelled, and I was just out of luck. They were not willing to share the proceeds or reimburse me for my expenses, as the swooping purchase had taken place outside the sale. I had sunk money into advertising, staging, labor and planning for the sale and was left out of the deal. I chose not to pursue any legal satisfaction, although I was hurt and felt wronged. I felt it best to forgive, let it go and move on.

Seller's Remorse

One day a friend brought us some items for a sale we were conducting. He arrived with some nice things but also had some badly mildewed cushions for patio furniture. I instructed my helper William to dispose of the moldy, smelly pillows. When I took William to his home near Shelby Park, I suggested just throwing the stinky cushions into the community dumpster.

That night, I got a call from the owner of the odorous items, saying he had changed his mind and wanted them back. Well, I called William at 9:00, collected several large flashlights, and got Jimmy to go with me. We met William at the dumpster in the projects.

William climbed in and Jimmy and I bent over the sides, shining lights into the huge metal containers, looking for those cushions. Finally he called from the darkness, "Mrs. D., here's one!" We dug around and found the rest of them, but we had learned a lesson. Never discard anything without checking. By the way, the owner never knew what a ride those cushions had taken and of the distress they had caused all concerned!

Sales Peril

There was a sale where a short, stout lady came in with the early morning rush of customers. In her haste she ran into a large glass top table and fell flat on it. I was summoned from the kitchen for help. When I approached the living room, there she was spread eagle on the table, backside up, yelling that she couldn't get up. It looked to me as if her knees had bent backward. I got a chair and had her lifted off the table as she groaned that she couldn't bend her legs. After lots of ice, coaxing and reassurance, we got her back on her feet.

A VAN-FULL OF BEES

At another sale, I unwittingly parked my van right over a hole in the ground that was home to some sort of bees or yellow jackets. It was hot, so I left the windows open and went on my merry way. When I returned, my van was covered with bees, both inside and out. Before I could back away, they swarmed and stung me on the head and arms. We had to call an exterminator for the bees and find some first aid for me.

BOING, BOING, BOING!!!

At one sale, a man bought a bed that was stored in the attic. I asked how he would get it through the small attic door and down the narrow stairs. There was no way it would fit. But he was unconcerned and said it would not be a problem. The next thing I knew, I heard a chainsaw firing up in the attic. I ran to find the man sawing the box springs in half. The roaring noise of the saw and the "boing" of the springs boinging out made quite a racket. When he was done, he cut off the saw and calmly explained that he would put it all back together when he got it home. It was his bed at this point and he had the chainsaw, so I wasn't going to question him now.

For Sale, For Funerals

Funeral directors have feelings too. Well at least they have stuff, and sometimes that stuff is no longer needed or wanted. This was the case of one funeral home in Nolensville. I got a call from the owner, who asked me to conduct a sale for her home and her funeral home, conveniently located next door.

We sold an embalming table, old bleeding vessels, and all the other morbid tools of the trade. I learned then that there's a buyer for most anything. I sold the embalming table for $150, later to learn the buyer resold it on eBay for $900; a new meaning to *passin' it on*.

Happy Little Pills

Personal items are just part of the job in the estate sales business. I have learned to turn a blind eye to some of the things found. I always err on the side of caution, when it comes to tossing things in the garbage. We were preparing for a sale, the owner was moving to Florida after his wife had passed away.

He had moved out of the house and asked us to sell it all, except for the urn on the mantel, which contained his late wife's ashes.
We put the urn by the front door for our client to take to his new home. He checked on the sale several times but somehow forgot the urn.

My standard procedures for the sale were well under way, as we cleaned up and set out tables. I told my staff to empty the medicine cabinet, as we do in such "sell it all" cases. I felt a twinge, as if something wasn't right about this, but shrugged it off and continued on with my merry work.

The day before the sale, our client returned looking very disturbed, searching high and low for something. He flatly refused to tell us what, he was looking for. He left in a huff and promised to be back.

Then it hit me, I had seen a bottle of Viagra go out with the rest of the medicine cabinet's contents. His secretiveness must mean he was looking for something embarrassing, maybe this!

I hurried out to the dumpster and somehow found the little bottle. I returned to the house and nonchalantly placed the bottle beside the urn in the front hall.
He did return as promised. He came in, snatched up the pill bottle, wheeled around, and was gone without a word.

Somehow, he still forgot to pick up his "wife" in the urn.

CHAPTER

12

BARBARA MANDRELL'S ROLLS ROYCE AND A LOAD OF HORSE HOCKEY

═══════

IT HAS BEEN MY GOOD fortune to work with celebrities from time to time. I have, for the most part, been blessed to work with stars that are kind and friendly. I am certainly aware that is not always the case in the realm of the well known. Barbara Mandrell, the beautiful blond country music singer, called on me to do several sales for her over the years. In one particular sale, she was going from a 23,000 square foot mansion to a house one fourth the size.

Barbara had a number of unusual things only the

affluent can afford. She had a helicopter that I attempted to sell to Chi Chi Rodriguez. I told him it was just perfect to taxi in top golfers and celebs to tournaments. I had a good time working with him. Chi Chi is one fun-loving character. He went up for a spin in the helicopter, and almost bought it for his golf course in Puerto Rico, but it wouldn't hold as many people as he needed to transport from the airport to the golf resort.

We also had a Rolls Royce for sale, which we posted on our business website: www.bernicedenton.com. I received a call from a man in Eminence Missouri.

He said, "Hello my name is Jim Smith, from Eminence Missouri. I want that Rolls Royce you got posted. Is it still for sale?" He said he'd called four times trying to reach me and sounded irritated. I said, "Why yes it is." He said, "I just sold $22,000 worth of horseshit and I'm ready to buy." I quipped back, "OK then Jim. You'll have to sell $3,000 more of that stuff if you really want that car. Maybe Santa will give you the rest!" I suspected he was putting me on. He quickly said in a thick Southern accent, "Oh ma'm, I am quite serious." With my long list of practical jokes, I was a likely target for retaliation. I thought for sure someone was playing a joke on me. I didn't think he had much intention of following through with his horse hockey plan. But by 5:00 the next day, he wired me $25,000 and the Rolls was his.

It turned out that Mr. Smith owned the largest trailblazing business in the Midwest. He purchased Barbara Mandrell's Rolls Royce as a gift for his young granddaughter. He ended up putting it in the middle of his riding arena under a huge dome. I told him I wished I had a grandfather so generous.

That evening I was in the clouds that things had gone so well. After the sale was over, I loaded the van with my staging items; lamps, tables, sheets, various accessories. Content with a week's work well done, I punched the gas pedal of my van, and heard the unnerving sound of stuff sliding on metal and on the ground. I had failed to close the rear doors of my van tightly, and out poured the majority of what we had just loaded up. I was mortified and had to stop traffic to pick up what I could. All I could do was begin unceremoniously loading the ousted items back into the van. Life has a way of keeping us humble; at least it does for me.

CHAPTER

13

GUN BARREL GREETING

━━━━━━━━

ONE OF THE LESS THAN glamorous parts of my business is waltzing into the middle of the occasional family quarrel and sometimes all out brawl. The rural Nashville outskirts are known for some real Hatfield-McCoy-esque relations in amongst the hollers and the hills, and I have had my share of dealin's with them onr'y as a kickmule, critters. It's my job to sell stuff in houses, so this puts me in a very intimate place in people's lives.

One cold day I pulled into the gravel drive out past the cow pastures at a home in Lebanon. It was a gorgeous, expansive farmhouse on a hill overlooking a lake on the property. It was apparent there was a great deal to fight over. The man had been quite successful in the music industry. The windows looked dark and the house was still. The appraisal was to be conducted for the homeowner, who was soon to divorce his wife who had left him for a younger man. It was a tumultuous separation, and the courts were well involved, as they had to be for the property settlement.

I approached the entrance. The glass storm door creaked loudly as I held it open and knocked. I made small talk with the soon-to-be ex-wife and her lawyer's two assistants, who were accompanying me. We waited, and then waited some more. It was windy and quite cold with the temperature well below freezing. I knocked again, this time much louder and longer than before. Still nothing, just the sound of the wind and the caw of a crow that stood in the front yard.

I lifted my hand to knock again when the pop of a deadbolt being released could be heard inside, and the door swung open in a fury. There stood my client's soon-to-be ex-husband, glaring at us from the house, squinting in the daylight. My eyes adjusted to a view of the dim interior, and I saw that he gripped a weapon, a shotgun. Its dark wood and oily barrel were poised menacingly between us.

I thought for a moment and then tried to calm him down. I told him, "We have come to help you and do an appraisal." He was tall and somewhat intimidating, but his anger seemed to be fading. He said, "I only want you to come in. No one will enter but Mrs. Denton. These other people have to go before we get started."

We were in the country, it was freezing cold and they had no transportation, as they rode with me. I didn't want to be left alone with this angry man, but I agreed and someone from the lawyers' office came and picked them up after they had been out in the cold for an hour.

I told him to put away the gun, and I would finish the appraisal. He cooperated and ended up being happy with my work. In retrospect, it would have been prudent to do an about-face to the car and call the authorities, but I forged ahead.

CHAPTER

14

SOMETHING
IN THE
FREEZER

———

THE JOLT OF A MIDNIGHT phone call roused
Jimmy and me from our slumber on more than one
occasion. Calls at this time of night were usually an
emergency, but seldom one that we were qualified to
attend. My husband, the good banker, Jimmy
Denton was often mistaken for the good dentist,
James Denton as listed in the phone book. Jimmy
would laugh and sometimes tell them to, "Take two
aspirin and call me in the morning!" and "Put a hot
poultice on it!"

But good manners prevailed for the most part and we
would direct them to the appropriate Denton, the

dentist. As it turned out, Dr. Denton passed away suddenly from a heart attack, and I was engaged by the family to handle his estate sale some years later. Once we put it all together, that this was the same Denton for whom we'd been getting calls all these years, I had to admit to the Denton family our occasional late night pranks. As an aside about the family, Dr. Denton's son, Jamie Denton, is an actor on the well-watched show "Desperate Housewives".

The house was mysterious and had an air of danger. We were told Dr. Denton had a huge collection of guns in the house. My staffer, Ed Arnett, found a wall that swung open to reveal a secret storage space. He pushed it open, revealing a large cache of weapons. I immediately informed the family and they gladly dealt with the find.

During the sale, many guests, my staff and I gathered in the large kitchen, conversing and milling about, when a customer, with her two children opened the door of an old freezer that stood in the corner of the kitchen. My faithful staff backed away, mouths agape, faces pale as the door swung open. The inquisitive woman stood there, pressing her face into the freezer while her children screamed. The woman shrieked, and Ed jumped forward slamming the door shut. No one said a word, or moved. I crept forward and slowly eased the freezer door open. I was praying a body hadn't been stuffed into it.

What I saw was cause enough for me to step back and catch my breath. In the freezer was a large boa constrictor, wrapped around itself spilling from shelf to shelf. Its massive head sat at about eye level frozen in a straightforward gaze. Its head was half as big as mine! I looked at the woman and my workers trying to think of something to say. The snake was most certainly dead and frozen solid. That truth seemed to provide little comfort to our horrified, now ashen customers, who were quick to exit the premises still looking as if they'd seen a ghost or... an enormous snake in a freezer.

Upon further inquiry we found out that the boa constrictor had been a pet of Dr. Denton's for 22 years. Dr. Denton had a predilection for snakes, according to his family. It was not out of the ordinary for him to travel to Alabama and return with cages full of live rattlesnakes. For the Denton family, snakes were just a part of life. The big boa constrictor lived in a large, glass-doored gun cabinet with a hole cut into the top of it, so he could come and go as he pleased.

The snake had been frozen for several years. The family was so fond of their father's pet, they had planned to have it stuffed and mounted, but that task had not been undertaken. He'd been placed on ice for the interim. The snake had expired shortly after Dr. Denton's passing. He refused to eat and was just devastated from his owner's death. So is this a case of a snake dying of a broken heart? Jamie, his son, took over the frozen serpent with a plan to have it stuffed. That snake almost took a few more with him during my sale. That's not one to *pass on*.

CHAPTER

15

PRACTICAL GOAT

THERE'S A
BACKHOE ON THE BOULEVARD

PRANKING VINCE AND AMY

SOME FRIENDS OF OURS, the Omans were masters of the practical joke. On more than one occasion we had fallen prey to their cunning ways and ended up consumed in the hilarity of a good prank. It's all in good fun, but it's more fun to be somewhere other than the receiving end of the joke.

Family friend, Bill Cate, Jimmy and I hatched a plan to spoon the Omans a taste of their own medicine.

Bill said, "I know where we can get a goat."
Jimmy chortled, "A goat, what can we do with that?

Well, we'll think of something. Goats are funny. Let's get it!"

So off Bill and Jimmy went to secure a goat from a farmer. Bill figured he would be okay with us borrowing it for a while.

We decided to stash the goat in Stirton Oman's station wagon, leaving it as a nice surprise for their return home. We crept up the driveway with the furry little goat on a leash. It was a small but stubborn billy goat that kept trying to butt us and made all kinds of racket as we made our way to the woody station wagon. We eased open a door and began to push the little goat toward the opening. His bleating grew ever louder as he effectively put on the brakes with his hooves. We pushed his rear and with a good shove from Bill and Jimmy the old billy jumped up on the back seat. He looked quite indignant over the whole affair. "Done," shouted Bill as he slammed the door and we were off.

We figured the Omans would find the goat in an hour or so and the bewildered family would be no worse for the joke than, "What on earth do we do with a goat?" Unfortunately, this was not what transpired. The Omans did not discover the hoofed character in their station wagon until the following morning. The goat had eaten the upholstery. The seats were torn and ripped and the shredded lining was dangling from the roof. A bit of carpet fuzz clung to the billy goat's beard, as he stared out the window at the family blinking back in disbelief at what they were seeing.

This was a bad joke. We had to pay to have their car reupholstered and cleaned. The goat ate the whole inside of our friends' car. Some pranks end up joking the jokers.

THERE'S A BACKHOE ON THE BOULEVARD

Somehow, Jimmy and I managed to tread the slippery ground between both camps in the practical joke business. Stirton Oman was hot to get back at Bill Cate, mastermind of the goat-in-station-wagon fiasco, and Jimmy and I were more than happy to play.

We decided to take this giant tractor thing that was on a work site just off Belle Meade Boulevard. Stirton was going to hot wire it, and Jimmy was to drive it down the street to Bill Cate's yard. So we headed over to the Belle Meade police station and informed them of our plan. (Now, this was a long time ago and would never happen or be allowed these days.) "We're not stealing it," we emphasized. "We're just sort of borrowing it." I am not sure they believed us or fully understood our plan. They soon received calls that a heavy tractor was rolling right down Belle Meade Boulevard in the middle of the night. Jimmy didn't know how to drive that thing any more than a rabbit and the big shovel on the front end kept dipping and heaving up and down. I thought he was going to dig up half the Boulevard.

We got to the Cates' house and Jimmy roared into the driveway and parked it in the back yard. We couldn't cut it off since it was hotwired, so we fled the scene as lights started popping on in the houses.

The following morning I drove by the work site and saw men in hard hats standing around looking puzzled. I pulled up slowly and lowered my window. "Are y'all looking for something?" I asked as innocently as I could. The foreman said, "Why yes m'am, somebody stole our backhoe."

I smiled, "Oh I don't think anyone stole it, I think someone might have moved it though. Go down to Parmer School and go up that road right beside it. I think you'll find it in a back yard. I am fairly sure I saw it there this morning." I rolled up my window, waved and off I went. Leaving a very puzzled foreman.

They did retrieve the backhoe. We held them up a little that morning but other than that, a completely harmless joke. Well, we also cost Bill Cates a good deal of beauty rest, since the machine had been hotwired and it took him half the night to get the thing shut off. That should teach him not to leave a goat in somebody's car... of all the nerve.

PLAYING A JOKE ON
VINCE GILL AND AMY GRANT

I was having a sale in Deer Park. I happened to mention to Amy that if she and Vince would like to, they could go over and see if they wanted to buy anything before the sale started the next day. So

Vince and Amy went over to check out the sale items, and they took a rug to see how it would look in their house. I went in the next morning, and the rug was gone. This gave me an idea. I thought, "I'm gonna get them." So I called the police, and told them I was doing a sale across the street from Vince and Amy, and they had taken a rug from the house to see how it would look in their's. "So," I said, "I want you to play a joke on them for me. Go to their house and inform them that a rug and all the silver are missing from my sale, and ask if they have any information on the items." Well, the police were not interested in playing along at first, but I was persistent and they finally said yes.
(Again, this was a long time ago and would never happen today.)

So they went to "investigate." Vince answered the door barefooted, and they explained to him about the missing items. Vince said, "I have the rug, but I didn't get the silver!" So the boys in blue asked him to come with them across the street and loaded Vince Gill (still shoeless) into the back of the police car. They pulled up with me standing on the front porch just laughing! Vince knew then it was a big joke and he swore up and down, "I'm gonna get you back!" Well, to date he has yet to prank the prankster, but I best not sell the two of them short. Who knows what plan may be in the works?

Actually, Amy's son did get me back. Matt Chapman and my grandson Tee Stumb loaded up my truck for Christmas Village. The night before the Village set up began, they snuck over and "kidnapped" the truck. I went out next morning, and my sleigh had vanished. I was shocked. Everything I was to take to the Christmas Village show was in that truck. I had an inkling the boys might be involved, so I called them and told them the story and said I was calling the police. Well, I called the police to report the missing truck, and they told me that if this was a prank, I had better find out because the pranksters would be taken to jail, no joke. When the boys heard this, they quickly returned my truck full of Christmas goodies.

ALLIGATOR IN THE BATHTUB

What happens when you hear that there's a live alligator in the neighborhood? Well, of course, if you think like me, you figure it might be a perfect prop for a prank. Well, when Jimmy and I found out that a friend had brought a baby alligator back from Florida, we were quick to ask if we could borrow it. As a matter of fact, when we asked, our friend said, "It's yours. Just keep it." With that, the alligator was complicant in our newest plot.

Our neighbors, Liz and Jim Bess, had asked us to keep an eye on their home while they were out of town. This made them an easy target for our kind of humor. We decided to put the 'gator in their bathtub right before their return.

When they returned from their trip, Liz screamed to Jim, "There's an alligator in our bathtub!" Jim said, "Oh, Liz it's just a toy." He began to drop water on its then still head to make sure it was a toy. The alligator raised his head and opened his mouth to catch the drops of water. Jim and Liz flew out of the bathroom, slammed the door and stuffed towels under the door to keep it from crawling out. All they could think to do was to take it to Richland Creek and let it go. I have not heard of anyone in the vicinity sighting a 'gator in the last twenty years, so I guess he swam off to some warmer climate, or maybe not...

A YARD FULL OF SNAKES!

I got a call. "Honey, come home immediately. Our yard is full of snakes." Our grandson Tee Stumb was playing in our yard, and came running to Jimmy for help. The yard was indeed full of snakes, fifty or more, Jimmy estimated. I said, "Call the police."

Well, when you call the police to say your yard is full of snakes, the police will likely say, as they did say to us, "This is a very unusual call. You need to call an exterminator immediately." By the time I got home, the snakes had all gone back underground or slithered away.

Our neighbors were building a swimming pool, and there had been some blasting. Since none of our friends claimed it as a joke, we assumed the explosions accounted for the phenomenon.

Incidentally, it was a long time before Tee wanted to come for a visit.

CHAPTER

16

Pet Replacement Business

Watch Out...
I'll Sell Your Coat!

Well, Whose Car Is It?

———

OUR DAUGHTER KATHY asked Jimmy and me to dog sit while they were out of town. I accepted for us and was glad to do it, but I didn't think the task entirely through. The dog was a rambunctious pet and our home was a place of constant activity. In the daily commotion of visitors and doors opening and closing, their dog made his escape.

We searched all over the neighborhood for the wayward pet, but it was to no avail. Kathy was incredibly fond of this dog, and I started to worry that she'd disown me for letting him get away. Jimmy and I circled the neighborhood, driving up every street calling the dog by name. He was just gone, vanished. I cried to Jimmy, "She'll never forgive me." In my despair, I hatched a plan to cover up the loss. "We've got to find another one." Jimmy looked at me with eyebrows raised. "What?" he said.

"We've got to find a dog just like theirs, so they'll never know." I made a call to the police station as well as the shelter asking if they, by chance, had a little black dog. It turned out a small black mutt with a white spot on its chest and no collar had been found sniffing around in a garage on Lynwood. I went to investigate.

The dog looked a great deal like theirs. "This one will have to do," I thought. I took him home and got out a black magic marker, held him still and began my alterations to make him a totally black dog. I told the replacement dog, "Now, don't look at me like that, you're not supposed to have any spots, and act like you've been here before." He just panted and licked his chops smiling. When I finished, the dog actually looked a lot like their previous pet. Unfortunately there was one problem. This dog left me a present in a back room on our green carpet, after just a few minutes of being there. Maybe he mistook it for grass. He was not housebroken, and Kathy's dog was. There was not time nor energy for a lengthy training period. I had to admit defeat, and we took the replacement pet to the shelter. But by a stroke of good fortune, we found Kathy's real dog at the shelter the very next day. I am sure Kathy is more fond of her mother than that spotted dog, although I am glad that truth was not put to the test.

Watch Out... I'll Sell Your Coat!

I was in full selling mode at a particularly well-attended sale. The cash register was ringing, ringing, ringing! The rush and rhythm of doing good business is an amazing feeling, so much hard work and planning all paying off. It must be how farmers feel harvesting crops from their well-worked fields.

A woman walked up to the cash register with a beautiful, black coat. We were puzzled searching for the tag on the thing. After a diligent search, I decided the tag had fallen off and set a price on it on the spot. The customer found it fair and another happy sale was made. As she departed, I felt an odd twinge and thought, "Funny, I don't remember that coat, seems I would, it being so new and stylish." I cast off the notion deciding one of my staff must have priced it in the fracas.

Not thirty minutes had passed when a woman rushed up to me. "My jacket! I can't find my jacket, and I know I left it right here!" She pointed dramatically to the very spot from where the woman had gathered up the just sold jacket. I had not only sold this poor lady's coat while she was merrily shopping at my sale, but as it turned out, her car keys went along with it.

I hoped the buyer would return once she found keys in the pocket but to no avail. I replaced the coat and the keys and apologized as many times as she would listen. The woman got the best end of the deal, as the brand new coat was far nicer than the one I accidentally sold!

WELL, WHOSE CAR IS IT?

One day Jimmy was leaving the post office, minding his own business, as he frittered through the stack of mail he had just retrieved. He reached for his keys and opened the door to his blue sedan as he read intently, not paying too much attention to what he was doing. He sat behind the wheel and inserted the key. At that moment a woman in the passenger seat said calmly, "Well, good morning. You don't look a thing like my husband. He did say he'd be right back." Jimmy jumped, so startled he could have hopped right out the window.

Later Jimmy recounted, "It's a wonder she didn't scream or call 911 or something. I'm lucky she didn't have a gun in her purse!"

Jimmy is not alone in his mistaking of automobiles, as I am seldom to be outdone. One day I was running errands around town in a car loaned to me by Byrd Cain, at that time owner of a local Buick dealership, while mine was being serviced. After an errand at the five and ten cent store, I hopped in the car and looked at the front seat. Puzzled, I was sure I had left a curtain rod on the passenger seat. "Who on earth would steal that?" I thought. I continued with my errands, leaving the mystery of the missing curtain rod to solve later and was home by 4:00 to get dinner started for the family. The phone rang and it was Byrd Cain, sounding strange. He asked me if the loaner car was with me. I said, "Of course, I'm looking at it in my driveway." A confused Byrd asked, "Oh, um, would you go out and check the license plate, if you don't mind?" I was getting perturbed, "Well Byrd, I'm busy with my three hungry girls hanging all over me, plus number four, baby Jim, is asleep in the buggy. This better be important." I reluctantly agreed and ran out to do as he asked. I checked it and was stunned to find that the plate was not a dealer's tag. Here sat a dark blue Buick Wildcat, looking exactly like the car I had on loan from Byrd, and the key worked, and I had driven all over town. I thought it was the exact car, but it was not so! My loaner had been a La Sabre and, to me, the two cars were indiscernible.

Byrd put me in touch with the lady whose car I had taken. Baby Jim was still asleep, and dinner was on the stove. I politely asked the woman, since her key fit my car, if she could please drive the borrowed car to my house and pick up her car. My home was between where I had left her with my loaner and her home. It made perfect sense to me, and I had children to care for. She did as I asked, but was mad as a hornet by the time she arrived, "You stole my car! The least you could have done was return it!" It turned out I had stranded her at the dime store in her house shoes. She had dropped off her children at 10:00 in the morning for baseball practice and tried to run just one quick errand in spite of not being dressed for an outing. It was now 6:00 pm.

I tried to explain to her what had happened but she would have none of it. My neighbor Ann Lipscomb didn't help. Hee hawing across the hedge, she chimed in, "Oh, she does this all the time."

The woman had called the police and I'm lucky they didn't find me driving all over town. Then her husband arrived and Jimmy soon after. Tempers subsided after much talk and many apologies. The car had been a Christmas present from her husband, and she was heartbroken when she thought it was stolen. I sent her a bouquet of flowers with a miniature car stuck in the arrangement. The card read, "Keep this with you, so you'll always have a car available." I never heard from her. I am not sure if she ever appreciated the humor of the situation.

CHAPTER

17

Selling Our Bed
with Jimmy in It
&
Other Items Not For Sale

"JIMMY, GET UP! THIS MAN
WANTS TO BUY OUR BED."

EARLY ONE SATURDAY morning, I opened my home for my own sale. My first customer arrived at 7:00 sharp, asking if I had a king sized mattress for sale. I thought for a moment, thinking of Jimmy asleep in our bed. It was king sized, and really, we weren't fond of it. We had agreed it was way too firm and had discussed getting a pillow top. "Why yes, we do have a king sized mattress for sale. Just follow me." I said.

I led the man back to our bedroom where Jimmy was still sound asleep. The man stopped short of entering upon seeing the mattress covered in linens and a rather large lump in the middle of it (Jimmy).

"Jimmy, Jimmy wake up. This man is here to buy our mattress." Jimmy is long suffering and so very patient with me. He vacated the bed and I went to work. I said, "Here take a look, it's for sale and it's still warm!" The man bought the mattress and box springs on the spot, and my very patient husband helped him carry it out and load it up. Thank goodness Jimmy has a sense of humor.

"YOU SOLD MY WHAT?"

George Gillett who, at the time was, owner of WSM TV and Vail Colorado ski resort, was moving from his Nashville estate and relocating to Vail. He called me to conduct his sale. I was just amazed by what people would buy and why. One buyer bought George's used mattress and said, "I want to sleep where a rich man slept." Maybe he thought some of his success would rub off on him. Ordinary items sold hand over fist just because George Gillett had owned them. I watched as a customer happily purchased a set of used golf clubs. I was struck with an idea. "We've got an old set of clubs down in the basement. Jimmy never plays with those. I'll bring 'em in and watch 'em sell!" So I did just that. I never said they were George's clubs, but I never said they weren't either.

That night, we went to dinner with friends. I was bubbling over about the sale, telling about all the things sold, and I proudly announced that I had taken those old clubs from the basement and sold them.

Jimmy, "You what? Those are the clubs I take when I travel." The look on his face was anything but pleased. He continued, "Did you at least look in the side pockets? Did you get my cashmere sweater out? And what about my shoes?"

In my haste and enthusiasm I hadn't checked the pockets in which he had several personal golfing items of which he had grown quite fond. The cashmere sweater, especially, was a real sore spot for some time. Someone bought those clubs and got a bonus. They probably walk around in that sweater thinking George Gillett wore it.

I heard some pillow talk that night. Jimmy is a wonderful and forgiving husband, lesser men would have long since called it quits! They would have "passed me on." I did replace all Jimmy's sold items, with ones better than he had.

CHAPTER

18

INVESTMENT CLUB

———

I AM BLESSED TO BE part of an Investment Club that doubles as a group of friends. We had gone on several trips together and this one particular trip was mine to plan. It was decided we would go to New York. Fifteen of us left out of Nashville, on a direct flight into the big city. We were scheduled to be there in the late morning. We had two limousines that were to meet us at the airport and wisk us away in style to our hotel.

Unfortunately, we encountered some bumps in the road, or rather in the air. The turbulence was atrocious. The plane lurched, dropped and shuttered as we closed in on New York City. Black clouds and the booming sound of thunder rattled the plane and its passengers. Some got sick on the plane and the situation grew ever more tense.

With a loud crack and flash, lightning struck the plane. Soon afterward the pilot came over the speaker system and announced we would be circling the airport waiting for a break in the storm to land. Around and around we went. We ran out of water and every thing else they had to drink was used up.

The pilot announced that we were going to have to land in Bridgeport, Connecticut. Once on the ground, we pleaded with them to let us off the plane. None of us wanted to fly anymore. They said if we left the plane, we wouldn't get our luggage until the next day, so we stayed on board and took off again.

The storm seemed to intensify as we circled New York again. We were bouncing all over the sky. They then routed us to Philadelphia and again, would not let us off the plane. We had no water or food or anything. Finally the storms let up enough so we took off yet again and made it to New York by 5:00 p.m.

We finally got out of the airport and made it to our limousines, that had been waiting for us all day long. So we had a huge bill to contend with. We didn't have cell phones back then, and they wouldn't let us off the plane to make calls. They took us to the Knickerbocker Hotel only to find that they had cancelled our reservations for being late. We had to fight to get rooms which they eventually worked out, but it was just wherever they could park us.

The next night we went to a play, but when we got to the booth to get our tickets, they informed me that the tickets had been for Friday night. I was the one who had made the reservations, and had told them the day I wanted the tickets for and had just assumed everything was correct with the confirmation. So all these women were dressed up and waiting to go in. The performance was sold out, and the ticket agents were adamant that we had missed our chance. I was trying to do my best to persuade, but I kept thinking, "They won't make eye contact with me." Eye contact is essential in persuasion. They finally figured out a way to seat us and announced we could enter. Everyone, especially me, flew through the door. They found places for fifteen of us to sit, but they put us all over the theater, one here and one over there. But we did get to see the play.

We went to dinner after the show at One If by Land, Two If by Sea. The lady seated next to me Babs Walker choked on her food. I called for help and someone gave her the Heimlich. She scared us to death in that restaurant.

One high point of the trip was a special luncheon held for us by Christie's. I had built a good relationship with them. Having friends there, garnered our bedraggled band a slice of sunshine. It was a proud moment for me, I was so happy to get a chance to share a benefit of my profession with friends.

Our comedy of errors and misfortunes had a cumulative effect on the group morale. Nevertheless, we ended up having a marvelous time in spite of all our situational disasters. Good friends can have a good time just about anywhere, but honestly this trip called that notion into question.

CHAPTER

19

NOT ALL ROSES

<hr>

A SAD OCCURRENCE

ONE ESTATE SALE left a deep pain in my heart. We had been given instructions to arrive on a Monday morning. The client gave definite orders that she was not to be disturbed, and that we were to prepare for the sale. We found a set of keys in the door lock and, upon entering, saw a purse on the sofa with money falling out.

We set to work as directed, placing our display tables and organizing the large items for viewing. With the preparations well underway, I had to leave for a trip out of town and knew my staff could complete the work. When they finished the initial set up, they called upstairs to inform the lady of the house that they were leaving. Hearing nothing, they went upstairs and knocked on the closed bedroom door on the third floor. There was no answer. After several tries and no response, they carefully opened the door and came upon a horrifying scene. The woman had taken her own life. In a panic, my workers called 911, and in their confusion, gave the wrong name for the deceased. She was an attorney and worked with a local judge, and my distressed staffer gave the judge's name. The news put out a story that the judge had died. We quickly straightened that out. The mistake was promptly rectified upon the arrival of the medics and the authorities.

I feel for my staff that happened upon this tragedy. It is the kind of thing you never forget. The strangest thing about the event was that it seemed as though she had planned it so we would find her body. Not all days are filled with sunshine.

A Scare at a Sale

A woman was leaving our sale with her arms full several large pieces of ornate glass. She hurried out the back and onto the patio, hastening to get out of the biting cold. As she made her way around the covered pool, she lost her balance and stepped right through the cover. Down she went with the glass breaking as she fell.

Customers and workers alike flew to her aid, and we extracted the now soaked and badly cut woman from the large rip in the pool cover. We bandaged her up and got her warm, and her daughter took her home.

It was an awful experience for everyone, but I am thankful she suffered no long term injuries. We thought maybe she was trying to walk on water!

A TERRIBLE CRASH

One woman was turning into the driveway of a sale on Franklin Road when a car came speeding over a hill. The approaching car was unable to stop and crashed into the side of the turning car knocking it into a telephone pole. The sound of the accident was terrifying, and we all went running out to the tangled mess. I thought the driver was dead when I saw her, but she was just unconscious. We prayed for her and directed traffic as best we could until the emergency crews arrived. I thank God she survived.

SAYING GOODBYE

We had been asked to look over some items a lady desired to sell and had made plans to visit the home to do so. We arrived and were met by the husband. With his assistance, we began filming items she had mentioned We made our way back to their bedroom, and there she was. His wife had died in the night, and was in the bed as if asleep. He pointed and said, "There she is, over there."

It took all I had to hold back my tears and subdue my shock at the discovery. The man had been unable to tell us she had passed. We quietly packed up and left as quickly as we could. He seemed so confused, I later wondered if she had also been his caretaker.

BREAKS MY HEART

I was brought in to what had to have been the saddest of circumstances. There was to be a sale for a family of three. Mother, father and daughter tragically perished in a car accident while on their Christmas vacation. A brother and sister-in-law of the deceased were unable to face the situation, but wanted the sale to go on. It was surreal, the Christmas decorations were still up. We were even left to explain to friends and neighbors the sad facts, as many were unaware of the tragedy.

TOO CLOSE TO HOME

There was one time that I feel my brush with death was close. Some of the details even now, must remain secret. I conducted a sale for an Iraqi man who was a big contractor in town. I remember him forbidding my people to enter a certain part of the house. One evening, I was at his house. It was the very night the U.S. initiated the bombing in Iraq. I remember him talking loudly on the telephone, possibly in Farsi or some other Middle Eastern sounding dialect.

Earlier, I had backed my car off his driveway and

was stuck there waiting for a tow truck to come and pull me out. It seemed like an eternity. While I waited, he walked through the house talking on the phone. I busied myself with what I could for the sale, and when I felt it was safe, I sneaked down the hall and peaked into the room deemed off-limits. To my horror, the room was full of metal canisters that appeared to be capable of holding some kind of gas. I heard his loud voice booming and quickly scurried away from the door.

Petrified, I took deep breaths hoping he wouldn't pick up on my newly acquired knowledge. The tow truck man finally arrived and freed me from what I now felt was a terrorist's hideout.

I called the FBI and reported what I had seen. It turned out that my client and his brother were making Sarin gas and shipping it to Saddam Hussien. In fact his brother was apprehended and named by the UN as one of Saddam's suppliers. My client disappeared shortly after the sale was over, and I am not sure what became of him. He never returned to that home again.

Lights Out

Moments before we opened the doors for a sale, a violent storm roared through. Lightning was pop, pop, popping. With one extra loud boom the lights went dark. Normally, my sales are in the day and in homes with windows so this would have been little more than a annoyance, but this sale was set up in the home's large, windowless basement.

We did the only thing we could do, we got out the candles! Then we went around the neighborhood and asked to borrow flashlights. Thank goodness we survived that one and didn't catch anything on fire.

CHAPTER

20

THE BASEMENT
OF (NEAR) DOOM

I AM CALLED ON OCCASION to conduct sales in homes of mysterious and reclusive people. These strange clients make the initial visit to their homes something of an adventure. One such sale was at the house of a man who was at the top of the "loner scale". I opened the door to the basement. We had been told that no one was allowed down there, not even the family, so we were most apprehensive about what we might find. I descended the green carpeted stairs with a flashlight. As I reached the foot of the stairs, I swung my light around, catching metallic flashes in every direction. I stood at the base of the stairs and, as my eyes adjusted, the shadow-covered shapes became objects.

The basement was home to a magical miniature train world. Tracks ran in every direction and every meticulous detail seemed to have been attended to. I ran my hand over the wall until I came to a light switch and flicked it on. The lights came up and the buzz of electricity could be heard in the switch stations of the antique trains. Countless engines, colorful cars and red cabooses lined the black links of track all the way to the walls of the large basement. In the center of his "sanctuary" sat an old organ which he must have played while admiring his trains. This was a train collector's dream, and he had kept it to himself for all these years. The sale and the collection would bring curious neighbors in droves to see the fantastic display. Train collectors in the area, hearing of the find, would be in attendance as well, but not before a slight delay.

Day one of the sale started early with my phone ringing well before I was out of bed. The daughter of the owner was calling to say she was at the home getting it ready to be put on the market after our sale was complete. She sobbed over the phone, "I've found a grenade left in the house. Dad told me they were all gone." I was in shock as the day before, my staff and I, along with my client, had been milling about going through things all over the house. I asked, "Is it real? Is it live?" "Yes, I am almost positive it is," she answered. I told her to call the police and got there as quickly as I could.

The FBI descended on the property evacuating my staff. They had a lot of questions for the owner's daughter; there was great concern that there might be other explosives hidden in the house. It turned out, he was a WWII veteran and this was likely a memento he returned with after combat. The FBI searched the entire house but found no other explosives. The grenade was removed from the property, and we were told it was detonated at a secret location.

The grenade had been positioned in such a way that the police felt it had been laid as a trap for anyone trying to get into his precious space. It was set precariously above the doorway of the very place where I had been pulling and shoving boxes around the day before. It was one of those unbeknownst brushes with death. What a way to go – to meet one's demise at an estate sale.

The FBI eventually allowed us to continue with the sale, but just then a TV crew showed up. They had caught wind of the dangerous find. The owner's daughter pleaded with them to leave, claiming they would ruin the sale, and to our amazement, they agreed and left without filming or reporting the incident. Not all surprises are antique trains!

CHAPTER

21

THE
NASHVILLE
FLOOD

━━━━━

THE FIRST OF MAY 2010 will long be known in Nashville as the day of the flood. Rain fell steady and hard for hours and hours. The weather report showed a dark green mass anchored over the mid-state. I was in Leiper's Fork where my business had been for four months. My quaint shop in the heart of the little rural community was buzzing with activity. Leiper's Fork was having a Guitar Fest and everyone was involved. All the shops were hosting exhibitions where some of the best guitar players in the world were to play, and collectors were to have their fine instruments on display. There were big white tents set up for various displays and for the food vendors. We were going to have a fabulous time, and a large contingent of the music industry was out for the event.

I was excited to play hostess in my new store. They had even scheduled Vince Gill to play that evening at the Leipers Fork arena. As the day continued on, the rain was relentless. The Harpeth River ran behind my shop and was rising to flood stage, and there were rumors of possible tornados. We piled into the basement of the Country Boy restaurant next door on more than one occasion, heeding tornado warnings. But we were determined to party on even as the waters rose and the rain fell. I even told all the entertainers and a number of new friends that they could all sleep at my shop. It was looking like none of us would be allowed to leave as the water was up over some of the roads. I had beds and sofas and the Country Boy had plenty of food. Why not just keep the whole thing going? The seriousness of the situation had yet to sink in, and as the day progressed the weather worsened. The police informed everyone that it was time to go.

Guests became nervous. We looked down the road and saw nine cars partially under water. The party was cut short, and most everyone rushed to go home. It was apparent this was not a normal spring thunderstorm. It was 6:00 p.m. I had been having such a good time with everyone, I had let myself get trapped by the rising waters. Police were cruising the area, and I was told I couldn't leave Leiper's Fork to go home. I was unaware of how quickly the situation had gotten dangerous until I looked out the window and saw a school bus with water up to the windows and those nine cars now almost completely submerged in swirling coffee colored river water.

The encroaching Harpeth River subsided briefly, and the police allowed me to leave by the Natchez Trace Parkway. I was probably the last person to leave the area. It seemed to me that as soon as I got out of Leiper's Fork, the storm intensified again. I crept down the Parkway to Highway 100. There were many miles between me and my cozy home. I came to the first of two bridges that cross the Harpeth River. The rushing river sounded like a giant waterfall roaring, far out of its banks, swallowing up the trees and the yards as it rushed along. The water was nearly over the bridge. There were officers on either side of the bridge, and they asked me where I was headed. By this point I was almost in tears. I said, "Home! I'm going home!" The officer looked at the bridge and then back at me. He shouted over the deafening roar of water, "Go!" and go I did. As I crossed the bridge, I wondered about the supports and the power of the water crashing into the structure. I let out a deep sigh and prayed as I edged off the bridge and went on my way. I was in for another breathless crossing as I traversed the second Harpeth River bridge. I made it across and by then, with night falling, I was growing ever more anxious to get to my home. My cell phone was not working, and if I got stranded, I had no place to go.

I came to Richland Creek, usually a babbling brook that runs through our neighborhood, now a muddy, deep, swirling river pouring out into yards, covering streets and filling culverts. I crossed the bridge on Jackson Boulevard. The creek was now roaring and angry. Water was coming over the road and rushing under my car. I prayed and squeezed the steering wheel tight, pressing down on the gas, as I felt the water slowing my progress, splashing up the sides of my car doors. I made it through the final obstacle, thanking the Lord all the way into my driveway. I was home and was overcome by relief seeing Jimmy and feeling safe.

The next day, Sunday, the flood worsened, and we couldn't make it out to church. All of Nashville was in a state of emergency. People were asked to stay home. Some who ventured out were washed away and lost their lives. Many lost their homes and possessions. The pictures on the news were of roads turned to rivers, people stranded, homes flooded and more flooding was predicted. A mile from our home, a couple trying to get to church, was swept away in the rapids. They drowned in the tragic accident. In retrospect, it was much more dangerous than I thought to cross the rising waters. I certainly have a new respect for the power of water.

Nashville is a city that rallies in adversity. The churches, along with civic leaders showed the true spirit of Nashville by coming together to clean up, rebuild, console, donate, and do what needed to be done to get our neighbors back on their feet. The efforts of its citizens sustain this wonderful city in a mighty way.

Footnote: Since this major event, I have had three of my own floods to deal with. Our gutters were overwhelmed in one storm, and we ended up with three inches of water in our house. Then, a broken water heater soaked us again. Finally, a flood at my shop/restaurant caused us to be out of business for three and one half weeks. I've seen enough water disasters and certainly hope they will pass on.

CHAPTER

FAITH
&
PHILANTHROPY

―――――――

IT IS MY DESIRE TO HAVE my work be a
ministry to others. I am content in the fact that my
work is where I belong. In the morning, I pray. I
pray that I will be led to the right places, people and
situations to further the Lord's work here on earth.
I do believe that we are called to be His hands, and
the "cups of water" we give to others are to be given
in service, in His name and for His sake. This belief
strengthens me in times of trials and brings joy to
most every occasion. The truth that there is a bigger
plan at work besides my own is always somewhere in
my thoughts.

We come here with nothing, we leave here with nothing, but it's what we do with what we've got that's important in God's eyes.

We are only the caretakers of our possessions. We all need to work at keeping our possessions from possessing us.

MY BUSINESS PLAN?

My estates sales business has been both lucrative and fulfilling. It's been a combination of God's blessings, hard work, and loving what I do. It is often said, "Do what you love and you'll never work a day in your life." I'm not sure that's completely accurate. After long days, I certainly know I did something and I am pretty sure it's called work. When I rise in the morning, I am filled with excitement thinking, "This is the day the Lord has made. I will rejoice and be glad in it." What will happen on this day? The Bible tells us to, "Rise and shine," and that is exactly my plan most days. My "work" occupies me and, I admit, it sometimes consumes me.

Several years ago, my son asked to see my business plan. "You can't see it. It's all up here," I said, pointing to my head. Jim was shocked. My business was created with an ever-changing plan. It could be titled "Whatever Works" or "Head above Water" or "Keep Your Customers, Staff, and Family Happy"...and maybe that's the best one. I must add, "Keep the Creditors Happy!" Such business savvy... Vanderbilt's MBA program may just come a'calling.

I encounter all types of people in my business, millionaires who haggle over every little thing, along with the bold and extravagant who say, "I'll take it! Now, how much do I owe you?" I enjoy the people and every part of the business, from the hauling of the priceless to the price-less, to the fixing and cleaning for a sale. I take measures to stay on top of the ever-changing market. I expand my knowledge by attending antique symposiums (such as Christie's Newport). I worked with the Phillip Morris Antiques Road Show for three years. I continue to learn and grow as a professional appraiser, antiques dealer, and estate sales manager. All the various elements of what I do and my love of family and friends make each day exhilarating and add up to a joy filled life.

Our early family years were filled with all the joys and challenges of raising children. I remained hopeful that someday I would get to work with antiques. I found that I had an ample supply of energy after caring for my family, and sought out ways to help others. I became involved with a number of charities, including the Fannie Battle Day Home (which helped working mothers with their children), Pi Phi Alumnae Philanthropies, Vanderbilt Children's Hospital, Stephen Ministeries and the Florence Crittenton Home for Unwed Mothers.

CRITTENTON CARE

Those were the days when there was a great stigma to having a child out of wedlock, and little help was available. Girls from other cities and towns and from Nashville as well, would secretly come to stay in the Crittenton home during their pregnancy, have the baby with good hospital care and recovery, and then return home. Whether they kept their babies or gave them up for adoption was their decision, and that information was confidential. In addition to our professional counseling services, board members personally helped the young women as friends, and gave them support in any way we could during their stay.

We raised money for maintaining the large home by hosting special events featuring celebrities of the caliber of Johnny Carson and Chet Atkins and sponsoring professional tennis tournaments for the MS Foundation. Later, we created and sold our special Community Calendars, which I had introduced to the group as a new idea for Nashville. The calendars listed almost all Nashville events for the entire year, even including school schedules and activities. That calendar quickly became a must-have item for young, on-the-go Nashvillians.

CHRISTMAS VILLAGE

In 1961, the Pi Beta Phi Alumnae were looking for ways to raise money to benefit our philanthropies, The Vanderbilt Bill Wilkerson Center, and the Arrowmont School in the Appalachian Mountains. Barbara Fridrich and I came up with an ambitious plan. Barbara was a dear friend and sister Pi Phi alum. Together we proposed the idea of the "village" to our sorority. It was no easy-sell, as no one had ever heard of such a thing. This was well before shopping centers were even thought of. Committees thought it wouldn't work, but Barbara and I persevered, eventually winning our sisters' full support.

Our plan was to create an indoor shopping village, with all sorts of arts, crafts, and merchandise, allowing shoppers to find unique gifts from many merchants for Christmas. We decided to sell tickets and invite food and drink vendors. Shoppers would be warm and comfortable, and be able to spend an enjoyable day seeking that perfect something for the holidays.

Barbara and I served as the first co-chairwomen and founders of Christmas Village. Local merchants and craftsmen were eager to take part and show their wares at the Village with ready-to-buy customers. The first year was a two-day event at the old Hippodrome and raised $1020. Christmas Village is now considered a premier consumer show in the Southeast. Our idea has been recreated in most major cities across the country. I suppose, in hindsight, we should have franchised it.

When the smell of Christmas trees is in the air, lilting Christmas carols fill hearts with joy, and snow is in the forecast, it is time for Christmas Village. Today, over 30,000 shoppers attend the four-day event which hosts 300 merchants from across the country. The Pi Phi alumnae have raised over $7,000,000 for Vanderbilt Bill Wilkerson Center millions more for our other philanthropies, notably the Arrowmont School. We have approached fifty years of Christmas

Villages. I'm loath to admit being old enough to have been involved in its inception, but there it is; history cannot be denied.

> *Ed.'s note: Berenice was honored to receive the Carolyn Helman Lichtenberg Award in 2010. This national award is presented to a Pi Beta Phi alumna who, "exhibits excellence and outstanding leadership in their career or volunteer service."*

Barbara Fridrich was a big factor in my pledging Pi Phi Sorority at Vanderbilt. She was my role model, friend and close confidant. Barbara's strong Christian faith and loving, caring ways made a huge impact on my life. I loved her dearly. She passed on in 2008. I will miss her for the rest of my life, but I am happy to say the fruit of her hard work on this earth continues to benefit others. May we all be so blessed to have the same said of us.

A SIGHTING

A story written by our good friend

as his Christmas message.

By Charles Wells

BELLE MEADE is a city within the city of Nashville. Rather more town than city, it is the enclave of the super rich the rich, and the would-be rich. Even so, despite the influx of new faces and trophy houses, or perhaps because of them, it remains a pleasant place to live. Homelessness is not a part of the scene, though many of its residents give both their time and money for the care of the homeless in the center city.

Accordingly, Berenice and Jimmy, two of our dear friends, were surprised, driving home from dinner about ten-thirty on a Friday evening, as they neared the juncture of Glen Eden and Jackson Boulevard, to see a solitary woman standing on the corner.

"She was just standing on the corner, holding a bag," Berenice said. "You know the corner. It's where the Beamans live, and the Andersons before them." In Belle Meade, the houses as well as the people and the dogs are apt to have pedigrees.

Slowing down to turn right, they could see her better. She was not young, her clothes were not stylish; she didn't belong there. She gave no sign that she was aware of their passing.

"I bet she's just waiting for someone to pick her up," said Jimmy. They heard a motorcycle behind them and both hoped that would be the ride she was waiting for. As they neared home, neither felt comfortable. She was clearly homeless; just as clearly she was stranded late at night where the possibility for help seemed remote.

They could not let themselves abandon her. So they turned around even before reaching home and retraced their route. She was still there, standing in the same spot, head proudly raised, apparently unaware of where she was, her situation, or its possible danger.

"Whatever you do, Berenice," Jimmy said, "Don't bring her home." This said because Berenice has a reputation for taking in stray people and caring for them, sometimes for long periods.

"May we help you?" Berenice inquired. Yes, they could. She needed a ride. She had hoped to get help at St. George's but no one was there. She thought perhaps she could find a place to sleep at Westminster. Would they take her there? She seemed oblivious to the fact that it was highly unlikely she would find anyone at either St. George's Episcopal Church or Westminster Presbyterian Church late on the Friday night before July Fourth.

They could see her clearer now in the light of the street lamp. She had a pretty face, and although her clothes were ill fitting and obviously old, she was cleanly dressed. She spoke in a cultured voice that carried an air of cultivation and respectability. She got into the back seat of their car, and they drove off.

Both Berenice and Jimmy were growing uncomfortable. Could she be a part of some plot, some extortion scheme, some drug deal? Were they being followed? As they turned right from Belle Meade Boulevard into Harding Pike, Berenice suggested perhaps they could stop in at the police station just here on the right and she could find help there. Visibly agitated, their companion spurned any help from the police and begged them just to take her to Westminster.

There, as expected, they found only darkness and locked doors. Both Jimmy and Berenice now felt responsible for her. They couldn't leave her there alone. Jimmy offered to pay for her to spend the night at a motel, which was agreeable to her, and they turned onto White Bridge Road to find one. A Days Inn was found on the left near Charlotte Avenue, and a room was available. The night clerk was clearly not happy to take in a homeless woman with only a bag and no address, but Berenice told him firmly that they were trying to help her and it was his duty to help her too. Jimmy gave her a little money for food the next day, and they drove home.

Along the way to the motel, Berenice had the opportunity to ask many questions, and the woman was forthcoming. Her name was Patricia Hayes.

She was from Columbia, South Carolina. She was an actress and had appeared in several movies. She had been married and divorced three times. Her first husband was an ophthalmologist, and she had two children by that marriage. Her mother and father and siblings were still living, but she had nothing to do with them. She had been abused by them all, husbands and kin alike, and the break was complete.

Her swollen ankles and well-worn shoes had been apparent when she got into the car. What was she doing walking around Belle Meade late at night? She had been putting flowers in the mailboxes, hoping someone would help her find a job.

Their sleep was troubled. What were they going to do with her in the morning?

Berenice was up early and on the phone. She called every "Hayes" in the phone book in Columbia, South Carolina, until she finally found one who acknowledged that he was Patricia's first husband. Yes, she was an actress. Yes, she had been married three times. Yes, she was from a fine family. Yes, she had two children by him who were now nearly grown. She had been given a house worth half a million dollars in her divorce settlement, but the money was long since spent. She had been a beautiful, fine woman until she "went round the bend" but he could do nothing to help. He didn't want the children to learn what had become of her.

Notwithstanding, he provided the phone number for her brother and sister. Her brother reported that everything she had told them was true, except the abuse. She had never been abused. That was a delusion that had developed when she became mentally ill. She had been diagnosed as bipolar, or manic-depressive. They had done everything in their power to help. They had put her in a private psychiatric hospital, but her mother had taken her out, and then she had turned on her mother.

In every subsequent encounter she had become angry, accusatory, and vituperative, and they just couldn't take any more of those scenes. If she asked for help, they would give it, but they could not go to her asking to help again. Her mother too was concerned, but she couldn't offer any help either, for she was caring for her husband, Patricia's father, who was dying.

Later in the day, they talked again with Patricia. She told them she had had a good day. She'd been out walking, and she had sat for a while under a tree writing poetry. Her brother had told them this was what she always said when she was at a low point.

What could they do for her? What kind of help did she want? She begged them to help her find a job so that she could support herself. She would be willing to do anything. Now acquainted with her history of erratic behavior and aware of her somewhat bizarre attitude toward reality, they both know she could never keep a job in her condition. Would she be willing to see a doctor? Would she be willing to accept help from her family? No was the answer to the first question. Never, the answer to the second. Clearly drawn to her, they reached out again and agreed to pay for another night in the motel.

Berenice and Jimmy do not give up easily. Bright and early on Sunday morning, July Fourth, they were back at the motel again. She was not only in need; they found her appealing. They could now picture her as she once had been. They could see a Patricia restored to her former self. They must find help for her. But who would help aside from her family, and they only if she would accept their help? They can't find her a job, and if they could, she couldn't keep it.

Berenice confronted her once more about her family. No, they had abused her, and she would never accept help from them.

"But you're homeless, and you've got to have help," Berenice said to her.

At this Patricia bristled. She would never accept help from them, and with this they sensed just a hint of her possible anger. Furthermore, she said, she was not homeless.

"But you are homeless," Berenice cried, "and we've just got to find a way to help you."

At this her eyes flashed in anger. "I'm not homeless," she almost growled, and Berenice backed off. They would pay for another night at the motel. They could do no more.

Although she had both their cards, they have heard nothing since from Patricia. She had told them that if they wanted to reach her, they could leave a message at St. George's where she was known. Indeed, she was well known there. She had apparently spent many nights sleeping in the chapel at St. George's which was open at all hours for prayer. She had been discovered one morning by one of the clergy when he arrived to celebrate early communion. And the clergy at St. George's also had done their best to help. They too had found her appealing, one of their tribe despite her talk of abuse and of the FBI and of the Mafia. But she had rejected everything they had to offer, and she had moved on.

She has been sighted several times since then, once early in the morning leaving the porch at Immanuel Baptist Church, once walking down Belle Meade Boulevard, once walking down Harding Pike carrying two bags. The police have been asked to keep watch to protect her from harm.

A psychiatrist might say that Patricia could be helped if she were hospitalized and given medicine. But the wiser among us know there is no long-term solution for someone like Patricia Hayes. She will accept help only for today and for tonight. Tomorrow is too far away. The most we can hope is that she, and others like her, will from time to time meet caring people like Berenice and Jimmy, and that, in her troubled passage, flights of angels will hover round and preserve her from harm.

a message for Christmas 2004
from Ann and Charles Wells

CHAPTER

23

Miracles Do Happen

ABOUT TWENTY-FOUR years ago my husband developed something called torticollis, a painful disorder of the neck muscles. We went everywhere looking for help, and saw neurologists, neurosurgeons, you name it. Jimmy's pain would be so severe at times, we would be out somewhere and he would tell me he had to go home immediately.

At the same time, our one-year-old granddaughter was discovered to have a tear or hole in her heart. She began to have numerous colds and slept excessively. Dr. Nancy Chase at Le Bonheur Children's Hospital in Memphis said that when Catherine was two years old she would have to have surgery. At Vanderbilt, the opinion was the same.

Enter my sister Jean Ann McNally with the suggestion that prayer and the laying on of hands might heal them. Delores Winder, evangelist and faith healer, came to Nashville and laid hands on Jimmy. She said, "You won't be healed right away, but if you believe, read your Bible, and pray incessantly, you will be healed."

At Belmont Church in Nashville, hands were laid on Catherine. She would go around saying, "Hallelujah" and "Praise the Lord." She got worse, and the surgery was planned for around Christmas, just before her second birthday. I had told the doctor that God could heal our baby, but she said to me, "I have never seen one of these situations reverse."

An ultrasound was done to prepare for surgery. Guess what! The hole had shrunk to a tiny spot, and the operation was cancelled. We knew a miracle had happened, and we rejoiced with tears and cheers and prayers of thanksgiving. Those two years had been hard to handle. Years later, this same doctor took care of our thirteenth grandbaby, Jamie Stumb in Memphis. Jamie suffered from a tear in her lung right at birth.

Meanwhile Jimmy was driving home from work, choosing his route carefully, as the muscle disorder made it difficult to drive. The pain became so intense, he stopped his car by the side of the road and cried out for God to help him. Suddenly, he felt a pain like a lightening bolt travel up his spine and out his neck. With that, the pain subsided and did not return. Within three months the miracle was complete. The full range of motion returned amid much prayer and thankfulness.

CHAPTER

24

LUNCH BUNCH

───────

SOME OF MY MOST TREASURED moments are when I'm with our Lunch Bunch. The Lunch Bunch is an "organization" of nineteen women. We are Mandy Barbara of Cincinnati, Judy Britton of Houston, Betty Brothers, Gertrude Caldwell, Berenice Denton, Ginger Driver of Columbus, Mississippi, Gene Elliot of Shreveport, Louisiana, Allister Estes, Cornelia Faust, Bebe Harton, Kib Huddleston of Murfreesboro, Kay Lazenby, Ellen Martin of Washington, DC, Mary Alice Quinn of Memphis, Judy Reed of Greenville, Mississippi (and Seaside, Florida), Gardner Smith, Peggy Warner (part-time resident of Cashiers, North Carolina), Ann Wells, and Martha Winston.

Charlie Wells characterized our happy band with the following—

The Lunch Bunch is the name given to an organization of twenty-two women who are linked together in a most unusual alliance. Although the group scoffs at intimations of its exclusivity, most members admit that they can still taste the sweet silver spoon first foisted on them in infancy. Begun when some of them were brought together for play by their nannies, the group began to coalesce at Parmer School, became the closer at Ward-Belmont/Harpeth Hall, and solidified at Vanderbilt.

The size of the Lunch Bunch is established now by general agreement at nineteen members and there has been no new member in some fifty years, nor are there plans for lowering that standards. The group is distinguished by having no officers and no by-laws, and proposals for action are accepted only by unanimous vote.

It is to be noted that, with the exception of one sad loss in 2006, most members of the Lunch Bunch are in their seventieth year, and are still in remarkably combative shape.

Lunch Bunch meetings are held at noon on the first Thursday of each month in the Iroquois Room of the Belle Meade Country Club where, it is rumored, eyebrows have been raised by other diners because of their raucous laughter.

Over the years, members of the Lunch Bunch have gathered from time to time in Beersheba Springs, Cape Cod, Cashiers, Cincinnati, New Orleans, and Seaside.

Their activities in those locales have been shopping, eating, telling stories, and laughing, though they cheerfully admit that their only definite purposes are to enjoy, encourage, and support each other.

The Lunch Bunch has the distinction of being the longest-lived support group in the civilized world.

Venerable Sage, May 4, 2006

CHAPTER

25

POCKETBOOK PRAYER

SOW & GROW GARDEN CLUB'S
TRIP TO EUROPE

═══════

THEY TRUSTED ME, and I had blown it. An empty feeling in my stomach began to grow and spread over my entire body. The pocketbook was missing. The little financial center for our trip had vanished, and it had been mine to care for.

The Sow and Grow Garden Club was on a European trip, and I was the tour director. Our band of thirty traveled and explored wonderous gardens, and took in the culture everywhere we went.

We were in the south of France, settled in a hotel in Nice. For a day trip to St. Paul de Vence, we traveled by bus to the ancient walled city. The group convened at a plaza for an outdoor lunch. I was documenting with my video camera and put packages and other things by the table.

When we returned to Nice that afternoon, I touched my shoulder, almost without thinking to check on the purse, which held the group's trip funds – $10,000 in various currencies, tickets, and even some jewelry.

I used a waist pack when I traveled and was unaccustomed to having a purse on my shoulder. I felt for it, and it was gone. I couldn't think of when I last had it. My mind was racing and I grew frantic.

I prayed, "God, this is a big one. If you help me with this, I'm yours forever!" There was a lot of praying.

Bruno, our Italian guide, called the restaurant; no pocketbook. I was flummoxed. This would be my ruin. My friends would all be upset, and this was a lot of money I had lost and was going to have to repay.

In an act of desperation, I asked Bruno to call the police. He shrugged. "Worth a try," he said. After a long conversation and then a much longer pause, his eyes lit up. "Yes!?" he said. "You have a black pocketbook? OK, we are on our way." And with that, Bruno was hailing a cab and talking a mile a minute. Our French cabbie drove us on the Super Bon at speeds up to 170kph! I thought we might not make it. The cabbie, Bruno and I talked the entire time and all at once. At one point in the ride, a bunch of papers got sucked out the window, and we had to stop and pick them up. "An American, a Frenchman and an Italian were speeding in a taxi..." sounds like the start of a joke to me.

We drove right through the walled part of the city, short cutting to the police station. Cars are not allowed within the wall, but there we went with people shouting at us, "No, no, no!" Finally, we got to the station. My hair was standing straight up by now, I am sure. I raced up the thirty steps to the entrance (I counted). I rushed in and quickly verified that the pocketbook was mine. I checked the various pockets, and nothing was missing.

My pocketbook had been turned in by M. Jacques Galles from Bordeaux. He had found it under the table in the plaza. The police gave me his number, and I called him, and through tears of joy, thanked him over and over again. I declared then and there, "I love the French!"

From there our group traveled on to Paris. One of our Sow and Grow members was Honey Rodgers, whose husband Joe Rodgers was the U.S. Ambassador to France. Honey invited our group to stay with them at the Embassy for a few days. It was the high point of a wonderful trip, so many good friends in such an elegant setting. Joe loved my pocketbook story, and asked me to tell it in detail.

One night Honey invited five of us to climb through a bathroom window to venture on to the roof of the Embassy. It was a foggy night and there were no railings, but she knew just who would be daring enough to go out on the roof for a spectacular view of Paris, complete with fireworks. That is when Honey labeled us her "five most dangerous friends."

When I returned home, my mind dwelled on the kindness of Jacques Galles. I sent him gifts by way of my friend Katie Knaphurst Reasor, who was moving to Bordeaux. She was like another child to me. She had lived with us while attending Vanderbilt. I invited Jacques and his family to the states. They did not visit, so I returned to Bordeaux a year and a half later to visit him with my daughter Julie and husband Mark. Katie was still living there and served as our interpretor. Jacques and I cried when we met.

CHAPTER

My Business
Here
On Earth

═══════

ONE THING I HAVE to remember in my business is that regardless of what *it* is, *it* is on loan. The fact of the matter is that stuff can control us; it can consume us, blur our focus and take our direction off course. I feel that everything on this earth, that we are blessed with, is on loan to us. It is not our stuff, it is God's… it's a nice loan but what counts is what we do with the "*it*" and with our talents. I look at my life as a life on loan. I am far from perfect. I know I'm a work in progress; we all are, but the older I get, the more I understand about this. We live here but not for very long… and there are more important matters than simply acquiring earthly treasures.

Now don't get me wrong, life's a balance. I like the fine things, and they certainly can make life exciting. There are rewards from hard work, and some of those rewards are right here on earth. Have you ever heard the saying, "They were so Heavenly minded, they were no earthly good?" Well, I know we have practical needs and families to feed and diapers to change and the list goes on and on, and as we grow older the list just changes. I don't claim to shy away from such, but I know there is more, and one thing is for sure, none of it is going with us. You never see a U-haul being pulled behind a hearse. Well, actually one time I did. The departed was determined to take it with him. But just like the pharaohs' tombs chocked full of golden amulets and jeweled trinkets, not one shiny piece of treasure followed across that great divide.

(E)STATE OF MIND

The business of material possessions is what I work with and enjoy, but it is the relationships and people I encounter that make it all worthwhile. In my years in this business, I have developed a following of buyers, many of whom I consider friends, who faithfully attend my sales. I have had them follow me as far as New Mexico and Ohio. They keep up with me, and I am thankful that they do.

There are times, however, when people come to my sales thinking I am deceased because my signs read, "Berenice Denton Estate Sale." They ask me, "How did she die?" I happily tell them, "I am feeling quite well, thank you."

An estate sale of someone who has passed on brings unique challenges for family members who, in many cases have come into some semblance of wealth that they never had before. This situation can create some unpleasantness between loved ones. Greed and contention creep in, and before you know it, there's an all-out family feud. It's my job to keep the peace, or at least some level of civility. I've learned to be a mediator.

Estate sales are not only for the deceased. I hold many sales for the living who want to downsize, declutter or cash in on some of their extra belongings. The difference between an estate sale and a garage sale comes down to value. If you literally are clearing out a few things stored away in the garage, then that is exactly what you have. Put a handmade sign in the yard and have at it.

But if you find yourself with paintings, silver, furniture, clothes, anything more than a rake and a pair of work gloves, let's call it an estate sale. Even old toys can be collector's items. I recommend getting a professional appraisal. Antiques are defined as anything over one hundred years old; these items are likely to have true value but not exclusively. Many appraisers can be hired either to price only or price and handle the sale. I find most individuals will over price their sale. An appraiser will know the market and be able to set a price in line with prices of similar items that have successfully sold in the area. It is almost without fail that a professional appraisal will increase valuation for a sale.

As a professional appraiser, there is a certain procedure for pricing items. I first ask if there is an original bill of sale for the item. I determine if a provenance is available, documenting origin and tracing ownership. Then I have to ascertain if the item can be sold as a set or if it is one of several pieces that can be sold individually. Sets of things sell for more as a rule. I check eBay and other sale sites for comparable items, performing due diligence, even enlisting specialists and authenticators if necessary. Then I set a value. Now, most things in my sales are negotiable. If I have an interested buyer, I'm going to do what I can to put them together with the thing that they fancy. It's all part of the fun at an estate sale. People barter, dicker, and haggle over most any little thing.

Paintings are items with which an appraiser must be extremely careful. For artwork of any significant worth, we have to be sure of the authenticity. We are taught to read the signs of age, to date frames and to recognize evidence of touch ups. One great way to check a painting for anything that has been redone, touched up or fixed is to look at it under a black light. Anything new will show up. I check for artist recognition and then follow the painting back owner to owner.

I have several authenticators for artwork in New York. This process is a lengthy and costly one, but one must be sure. I recently had a client with a portrait of Rembrandt; it was thought to be a self-portrait, a true masterpiece in every sense of the word. After much deliberation, on line research and trips to New York, the painting was traced to the hand of one of Rembrandt's students, a very impressive piece, but not a master's work. This is why provenance is so important, not only for art but for any historical piece or antique of great value. It reduces the need for such investigations.

There are reproductions of art, pottery, silver and most any antique. The fakes have gotten so good, we are wary of anything without authentication. There are even some pieces of "fine" crystal coming out of Japan with etchings that are almost indiscernible from the real thing.

So, having the provenance, which is the history of the piece, provides authentication and the backing that allows an appraiser to price an item correctly. An item with historical significance must have with it proof of such. Alleged facts are worth nothing; one has to have factual evidence for the piece to be able to hold value based on its past. Now there are occasions, rare occasions, when fine art, and valuable documents and such have ended up tucked away in attics for decades only to emerge as treasures providing a fortune for the owner. This is why estate sale work is like hunting for buried treasures, we never know what will turn up.

Appraising always presents new challenges. One of my most complex appraisals was for West End Methodist Church. Valuing items, such as stained glass windows and a basketball court expanded my expertise. I try to stay current by taking classes and reading everything I can get my hands on and keeping up with Appraisers' Association of America news and other on line sources.

Placing a value on an antique or collectible is complex. Price guides are just that - guides. Often the prices listed are at the upper end of a range. A novice can field check the price listed for their item by researching antique malls, shops, and shows and checking months of internet sales. Condition must be comparable when comparing valuations. The professional appraiser, who can evaluate condition, spot reproduction and refinishing, who knows the market and has a notion of comparables, can often date a piece, price it with a realistic retail figure, and effect a sale while the amateur is still researching. It is an art and a science and experience matters.

Jewelry is one thing often overlooked by families in estate sales. Mixed in with costume jewelry, we unearth antique broaches, rings, and pendants oftentimes mistaken for little more than something for young girls to have for playing dress-up.

As far as what's selling currently, gold and silver, especially old sterling silver, are huge, and this boom is in full bloom. I have gotten wind of another trend. The Chinese elite are buying art, diamonds, porcelain, anything that could easily be taken with them if they have to make a fast exit.

As a rule, I try not be a buyer at my own sales. It is a conflict of interest to be both the appraiser and the buyer. Be wary of any appraiser who sets a price for you, and turns around and offers to buy it. It is not uncommon to get up to three appraisals on high dollar items.

The sale itself starts with the process of sorting,

organizing and pricing. Then we focus on staging. Eye appeal is key. When customers come in the door, it must be attractive and inviting. We put our best pieces where they can be seen right away, and we cover things that are not for sale. It never fails; they always want to buy what's not for sale. The house must be cleaned thoroughly. I tell my customers that we rarely clear out attics. I had an employee's feet and legs break through a ceiling while in an attic preparing things for a sale, and she was left with a nasty bruise. This incident, coupled with the constant heat and spiders, make attics a place that we just don't want to frequent.

Being in the estate sale business puts me in close proximity with people's lives, whether they are on earth or have moved on. I get a sense of who they are (or were), what books they liked, if they were spiritual, if they were loved by their neighbors, and in some instances, if they were alcoholics. I have found basements full of bottles. When we go in, there's really no telling what we will find, but my staff is never allowed to put names to the tales. We are hired in confidence and it is something we keep.

One time $5000 worth of Confederate bills fell from a hollowed out book. It would have been equal to half a million dollars at this time. Sometimes we find, well, personal things. At one sale my staff found several dozen, two-foot tall erotic statues in the estate. By the time I arrived at the sale, they had already sold several of them. They were displayed for all to see and were most embarrassingly explicit, not artistic. I had them taken out of the sale; they really were awful!
I tell my people to dispose of anything that will

embarrass the family. I want the last image of the departed to be wonderful. I am working for the family, and I want to leave their memories as good ones. My goal is to make everyone I am around happy. I want the buyers to get a good deal, and I want the sellers to get a fair price too. It is a balancing act.

I am a mediator for the family. I try to keep both sides happy. I think the ability to stand between two quarreling camps is a gift from God. I just tell them if they don't get it done, it's going to cost big bucks- and they're fighting over bucks, so I say, "Let's work it out." It's a simple matter of getting them both in a direction and keeping either side from digging in their heels or getting too offended.

I figure I've only got a little time. I've got a lot of work to do before I go. I want to stay on course. I have to walk the talk! I have had a wonderful life. I hesitate to say it because it sounds like bragging, but it is true. Now I've had some hard bumps in the road, but they have all worked together as blessings, even the bad times. That is how I look at life-it all amounts to blessings in some way. God uses it all. I would like to share this: get over the little things, the big things are what are important. Don't get bogged down in pettiness. Look at the goal that isn't here on earth, and my goal is to go there, and that is where I'm going. Climbing the mountain little by little. My grandmother would often say, "You can catch more flies with honey than with vinegar." Be kind as you climb. Just pass your love and kindness on.

ANTIQUES
ADDENDUM

ANTIQUES &
COLLECTIBLES

———————

Finding collectibles in the attic is both art form and treasure hunt with a fair degree of technical knowledge being a key ingredient.

One generation's everyday items, or even dime store purchases can be another generation's treasures.

1. The toys we played with
2. The clothes we wore
3. The cars we drove
4. The dishes we ate out of
5. The furniture we bought
6. The crystal, jewelry, linens, and more

These things have become "collectibles" in today's market, but in time, they will be antiques. An antique is usually an item that is at least 100 years old. This standard was set in the 1960s for purposes of defining which imported objects would be exempt from import taxes. A more traditional definition defines an item as "antique" if it was made before the 1830s era of mass production. In addition to the age of the piece, original character, condition, rarity, and provenance determine price.

In the 1950s Fostoria crystal or carnival glass could be bought at "dime stores" like Woolworth's and McClellan's. These collectibles now bring sizable dollar amounts at my sales.

The sign in front of one of my shops reads:
Come in and buy what your grandmother threw away
Handwork is one particular treasure that may often be overlooked. Women took pride in producing "linens" for the household. Pillowcases and sheets were adorned with embroidery, crochet and tatting. Dishtowels, aprons, tablecloths and napkins were sewn and embellished by hand. Even handkerchiefs were often made, not bought. Quilts were pieced or appliquéd and coverlets were hand woven.

BEWARE THE EMOTIONAL BUY

I once sold a Vanderbilt yearbook with Dinah Shore's picture in it for $375. The purchase was preceded by an all out bidding war for the item that I had expected would sell for much less. If you find yourself emotionally attached to an item, be aware that in the heat of the moment, you may pay much more than it is worth in terms of fair market value.

The Value of Paintings

1. Is the work signed by the artist?
2. Is the artist well known?
3. If the art is framed, is the frame original?
4. What physical condition is the painting in?
5. Has the painting been repaired?
6. Does the art have any historical significance?
7. Does the piece come with a provenance?
Provenance refers to the painting's history and/or artist's biographical information.
8. Is the piece a gyclee or some other type of reproduction?

When considering buying a painting that has been appraised, ask...
1. What is the fair market value? This value reflects the price of the painting on the open market, not necessarily what an individual might be willing to pay.
2. Was the appraisal conducted by a certified and unbiased third party?
3. Was the appraisal conducted within the last three years?

Rules of Antique Care

1. Clean Gently and Sparingly
The rich patina of a Roycroft copper lamp adds to its desirability. Shine it up and and hurt its value. However, careful washing of depression glass can make it more appealing.

2. Refinishing/Cleaning Furniture

Removing the original finish from antique furniture can be a costly mistake. The rule is, "less is more" with fine pieces. Usually a gentle cleaning will be adequate.

3. Exposure to Sunlight

Cracking textiles, fading old papers, and melted early plastics are all dangers associated with the sun's damaging rays. Keep such items out of direct sunlight and heat.

4. Amateur Restoration

Minor fixes are ok. Sewing on the eye of an old doll or supergluing a rhinestone back into a broach will be fine. More involved restorations; painting, carpentry, framing, etc. should be left to professionals, if at all.

5. Storage

Heirlooms and treasures should be kept away from heat and moisture. A good rule of thumb is, "If you are comfortable, then they are comfortable."

DATING FURNITURE

This is such an important consideration for so many that I want to offer you some markers for helping determine the age of furniture, art, and silver.

CONSTRUCTION EVOLUTION
WOOD

Patina is a natural buildup and is not easily faked.
In 17th century furniture, boards were laid so grain
ran from front to back. By 1789, grain ran from side
to side.

CONSTRUCTION
IN THE 17TH AND 18TH CENTURIES

- Mortice and Tenon were held by pegs or
dowels.
- Drawer linings of oak or pine were ¾" thick;
then in the 18th century, ¼" was standard.
- Dovetails were coarse and large early, and
progressively finer after the 18th century.
- Drawer bottoms were dry and untouched with
slight gaps between boards due to shrinkage.
- Runners were on dust boards between drawers
in the 17th century; later furniture had thick
linings with channels cut with runners in the
carcass sides. Starting with the Queen Ann
period, runners were placed underneath the
drawer, at sides, and ran on bearers placed
inside the carcass.
- Fronts in the 17th century were molded or
embellished with simple, raised decorations,
often geometric forms. 18th century fronts were
flat to accent the hardware and were neatly
finished, with molding such as quarter round or
beaded styles.
- Handles – early, they were held on with "split"
pin. In the 17th century, nuts and bolts secured
handles. Nuts were circular in the 18th century,

hexagonal in the 19th century.

•Locks were secured with handmade iron nails in the 17th century, with steel screws in the 18th century.

•Nails - Before 1786, all were handmade; after 1786, usually machine cut but hand finished. After 1800, machine cut, square and blunt and after 1890, machine made.

•Screws - handmade of brass or iron, had blunt ends, flat heads and irregular spirals before 1690. By 1800, screws were machine made with flat heads but they were more perfect in shape.

•Carcass - The inside walls should be "dry and "untouched", the underside dry and roughly hewn. The back, consisting of three or four backboards, sometimes is chamfered off at the edges and roughly nailed on. By 1850, more attention was given to finished backs of paneled construction but not polished. Later, backs were attached with countersunk screws.

DATING PORCELAIN AND POTTERY

Makers' signatures are most helpful in determining the age of porcelains and pottery pieces. When there are no marks, compare old to new by look, feel and weight.

•Older dishes are heavier than newer ones

•Older dishes often have no rim on the bottom

•Wares that have a foot rim on the bottom usually indicates a 19th century origin. An unglazed foot rim indicates origin prior to 1850.

•3 small marks – "spur marks" - on the face caused by a 3-pronged piece used to separate items during the firing were common until 1825.

Dating Marks

Between 1842 and 1883, the English used a "diamond" shape with this information:

Above the diamond was the "class" – metal, wood, glass. At homeplate, the year; 1st base the month, 2nd base the parcel number, 3rd base the day of "construction! In 1884, "RD" for "registered," was added to the center of the diamond. Numbers run from 1 to 548,920, larger after 1909.

After 1868, placement of the information changed:

Class was still above the diamond, but day was at homeplate, parcel number was at 1st, month at 2nd and year at 3rd.

- 1850: trademarks became fancy.
- 1880: LTD introduced
- 1885: Trademark used
- 1891: U.S. law required country of origin be stated
- 1914: "Made in (country)" became U.S. Law. Paper labels were sometimes used and therefore missing. Also, items may be older than the mark, as the mark may have been applied to an item years after it was made in order to import it into another country.

SILVER MARKS

Hallmarks for sterling were developed in England in the fourteenth century to identify silver content as percentage silver and copper per 1000 parts. The English sterling, meeting standard for the correct percentage of silver, was identified with the Leopard's head. In 1544, the Lion passant, facing left, right paw raised, was adopted. The stamp of the ruling monarch denoted the sovereign at the time of production, the "letter" mark for the year, with the maker's initials last.

U.S. MARKS

Before 1700 U.S. silver workers used initials to denote the maker and had marks other than initials. They used pressed pictures of eagles, a hand, a star. In 1860, the word "Sterling" was used. "Coin" was used to identify 900 parts sterling per 1000 parts. Most American silver will be stamped "Sterling". American Sterling silver is a top seller right now, especially if it is stamped Sterling.

SILVER PLATE

By 1830 electroplating developed and was often stamped "A1 plate." Triple, Quadruple or "ESPN" is electroplate on nickel. "ESPW" is electroplate on white metal.

GLASS DATING CHART

1715 - Flint glass developed in U.S.

1771 - Cut glass introduced in America:

1771-1830 – early period

1830-1880 – middle period

1850 - "rich cut" – deep cuts with
thicker glass using wheel of flat edge,
mitered edge and convex edge

1870 - curved miter wheel expands designs

1880-1815 – Brilliant Period

1827 - Pressed glass invented in the U.S.

1849 - Pattern glass developed

20th C - Art Nouveau

1930 - Art Deco

RECIPES

A Few of my
Favorite Things

═══

Cooking leads to sharing, love and laughter. This bonding agent for friends and family is high on my list. Here are a few of my very favorite recipes. Isn't it telling how we always gather in the kitchen?

Southern Tea Punch

8 cups water
1 family size or 4 regular size teabags
3/4 cup sugar
1/2 cup orange juice concentrate, thawed
1/2 cup lemonade concentrate, thawed
One drop cinnamon oil or one cinnamon stick
8 lemon slices and a splash of fresh lemon juice
8 sprigs fresh mint

Bring 4 cups water to a boil in medium saucepan. Remove from heat. Add teabags and cinnamon to the hot water and let stand for 5 minutes. Remove teabags. Stir in orange juice and lemonade concentrate. Pour mixture into a pitcher and add the remaining 4 cups of water. Discard cinnamon stick. Chill.

Garnish each glass of iced tea with lemon slices and fresh mint.

Tennessee Hot Chicken Salad

3 cups cooked chicken
1/2 cup chicken broth
2 cups celery
1 cup salted almonds
1/4 cup pimento
2 Tbs. lemon juice
1 Tbs. onion juice
1 1/2 cups Hellman's mayonnaise
1 tsp. salt
1/4 tsp. pepper
1 cup crushed potato chips
1/2 cup grated cheddar cheese

Place in casserole and heat at 450 for 15 minutes.

Sweet 'N Sour Carrots

2 bunches carrots
1 can condensed tomato soup
1/2 cup salad oil
1/2 cup sugar
1 tsp. Worcestershire sauce
1/4 cup vinegar
salt, pepper to taste
1 green pepper
1 jar cocktail onions or freshly chopped onion

Cut carrots crosswise and cook until tender. Mix other ingredients and add to carrots. Refrigerate overnight.

Cook slightly to heat. Serve hot.

White Chili

16 oz. white beans
6 cups chicken broth
2 cloves garlic, minced
2 medium onions chopped
2 Tbs. olive oil
2 4oz. cans green chilies (mild)
1 1/2 tsp. cumin
1 tsp. oregano
1/4 tsp. cayenne pepper
4 cups cooked chicken

Combine beans, broth, garlic and one of the onions. Bring to a boil and simmer for 2 1/2 – 3 hours.

In a sauté pan, combine oil, onions, chilis, cumin, oregano, cayenne. Saute til onion is clear. Add, along with the cooked chicken, to the broth and beans once beans are thoroughly cooked. Simmer for 10 minutes and serve.

Frozen Fruit Salad

2 cups heavy (whipping) cream
2 cups cranberry –orange relish
2 cups crushed pineapple, drained
1 cup Hellman's mayonnaise
1 cup powdered sugar
16 oz. softened cream cheese (set out of refrigerator ahead of time to soften)
1/2 cup chopped nuts (optional)

Whip whipping cream to soft peaks. Mix rest of ingredients and fold in whipped cream Freeze in individual cups or in a dish to be cut into squares. Cover and freeze.

Christmas Eggnog Cake

This is a no-cook recipe. I am told the Bourbon "cooks" the eggs. I always try to use the best quality eggs for any recipe, especially this one.

4 packages Lady Fingers, split
1 box Confectioner's sugar
1/2 lb. butter, softened
6 eggs separated
8 Tbs. Bourbon
1 cup chopped nuts (optional-I use toasted pecans)

1 pint whipping cream for icing

Cream softened butter with Confectioner's sugar. Add Bourbon to egg yolks and whisk together. Beat egg whites until stiff and fold into yolk mixture. Fold in nuts.

Line a large bowl with Lady Fingers. Pour in the mixed ingredients, cover and refrigerate overnight. Invert bowl over a serving plate and loosen the cake onto the plate.

Beat the whipping cream, seasoned with a sprinkling of sugar and a dash of vanilla.

Ice cake with whipped cream. Refrigerate.

When ready to serve, add a sprig of fresh holly for a festive touch.

Southern Lemon Squares

2 sticks butter
1/2 cup confectioners sugar
2 cups flour

Mix ingredients by hand and press into a greased
9 x 13 pan. Bake at 325 for 20 minutes.

2 cups sugar
1/4 cup flour
4 eggs
1 Tbs grated lemon rind
1/2 cup fresh lemon juice

Mix all 5 ingredients. Pour over baked crust. Bake
25 min. more. Sprinkle top with powdered sugar.

Southern Tomato Pie

Pre-bake one pie crust in a 9 inch pie plate according to
directions. Deep dish is best.
3 medium red tomatoes and 1 yellow and 1 green tomato
      or 5 red tomatoes
1 medium onion thinly sliced
6 slices bacon diced
1/2 cu mayonnaise
1 egg beaten
1/3 cup shredded Parmesan cheese
1 cup grated cheddar cheese.

Chop tomatoes and drain on paper towels. Sprinkle
with salt, let stand 20 min. Saute bacon with onion.
Drain and spread on the cooked crust. Add tomatoes.
Stir mayonnaise, egg and cheeses together and
spread on top. Bake at 375 for 30 minutes. Let stand
a few minutes before slicing.

Petits Pots de Creme (4 servings)

1 cup light cream (Half and Half)
1/4 cup sugar
1/8 tsp. salt
2 sq. semi sweet chocolate
2 egg yolks

Combine cream, sugar, salt and chocolate in top half of double boiler. Heat over simmering water, stirring constantly until chocolate melts and mixture starts to thicken.

Whisk egg yolks slightly in bowl. Slowly stir in some of the hot mixture to temper the eggs. Stir back into the mixture in top of double boiler and cook one minute, stirring constantly. Pour into petits pots or custard cups. Chill. Serve with garnish of whipped cream, a dash of cinnamon, and/or grated chocolate.

Pimento Cheese

1 lb. of NY Sharp Cheddar Cheese
1 cup grated pepper jack cheese
Jar of pimentos chopped
1 tsp. grated sweet onion
Several drops of Lea & Perrins Worcestershire Sauce
Hellman's mayo to mix
1/2 tsp. Maxine Chili powder

Chocolate Pie

1 1/4 cup sugar
1 1/2 cup milk
3 Tbs. cocoa (Hershey's)
3 Tbs cornstarch
Dash of salt
3 egg yolks - beaten

In top of a double boiler, mix sugar, cornstarch, cocoa and salt and stir. Add milk (1 cup), add beaten egg yolks – add rest of milk – stir while cooking. When mixture thickens add 2 Tbs. of butter and 1 tsp. of vanilla. Stir 1 min. more over medium heat.

Cool and add to baked pie crust – (I like Mrs. Smith's). Add seasoned (real) whipped cream and shavings of Hershey's chocolate bar or Heath bar.

Lemon Chess Pie

2 cups sugar
1 Tbs. flour
1 Tbs. cornmeal

Add one stick melted butter
4 beaten eggs
1/4 cup milk
1/4 cup lemon juice and 1 Tbs. grated lemon peel

Pour into pie shell.

Bake at 425 for about 5 minutes. Reduce temperature to 350 and cook until set.

Seafood Bisque

1 can tomato soup
1 can cream of mushroom soup
1 can split pea soup
1 can dry sherry
1 can cooked crabmeat, or another seafood of choice
1 can half & half or heavy cream

Mix together and heat but do not boil.
Good for lunch served with a salad and bread.

Chile-Corn Dip

2 large blocks Cream Cheese
1 #10 can (12 cups) corn niblets
2 cans chopped green chiles, drained
2 small onions chopped
2 sticks margarine
1 cup milk
Salt, pepper, cayenne to taste

Grated cheese for garnish

In a pan over low to medium heat, cut up cream cheese and margarine and heat together to melt. Stir in milk. Add drained corn, chiles and chopped onion. Heat and stir until blended. Add seasonings and top with grated cheese.

Apricot Bars

2/3 cup dried apricots
1 stick butter softened
1/4 cup granulated sugar
1 cup flour
1/3 cup flour
1 cup brown sugar packed
2 eggs
1 tsp. vanilla
1/2 cup nuts (optional)
1/2 tsp baking powder
1/2 tsp salt
Confectioners sugar to dust top

Simmer apricots in enough water to cover for 15 min. Drain, cool, chop.

Mix the 1/4 c. granulated sugar, butter and 1 cup of the flour together. Mix to the consistency of coarse crumbs. Press into a greased 8-inch square pan.

Bake for 25 min. at 350.

Mix chopped apricots, brown sugar, eggs, nuts, baking powder, the remaining 1/3 cup of flour, salt and vanilla. Pour mixture over the cooked crust and bake another 25 minutes.